PROFILES
IN
LEADERSHIP

ROBERT W. CRAWFORD
RECREATION AND PARK
HALL OF FAME

COMPILED AND EDITED
BY

CHARLIE E. HARTSOE

M. DOUGLAS SANDERS

MEREDITH BRIDGERS

ISBN-13: 978-1-57167-539-2

Supported by a grant from the Naitonal Recreation Foundation.

Publishers: Joseph J. Bannon & Peter Bannon
General Manager: M. Douglas Sanders
Editors: Charles E. Hartsoe, M. Douglas Sanders, & Meredith Bridgers
Production Manager: Jose Barrientos
  - Cover Design
  - Interior Design
Printed in the United States of America.

Sagamore Publishing, L.L.C.
804 North Neil Street
Champaign, Illinois 61820
www.sagamorepub.com

Library of Congress Control Number: 2007930275

Dedication

This book is dedicated to the men and women, both citizens and professionals, who have devoted their lives to enriching the lives of others through recreation and parks. *Profiles in Leadership* tells the story of 34 leaders who serve as inspiration to the future leaders of recreation and parks.

TABLE OF CONTENTS

EDITORS'
BIOGRAPHIES

Charles E. Hartsoe, Ph.D.

Charles E. Hartsoe is a Life Trustee of the National Recreation and Park Association. He holds a Ph.D. from the University of Illinois and has taught at Illinois, Pennsylvania State University, Temple University, and is a Professor Emeritus of Virginia Commonwealth University. Hartsoe is a charter member and past-president of the American Academy of Park and Recreation Administration. Following his academic career, he served as executive director of the National Recreation Foundation until his retirement.

M. Douglas Sanders, CPRP

Doug Sanders is the general manager of Sagamore Publishing and maintains an active membership with the National Recreation and Park Association and the American Alliance for Health, Physical Education, Recreation and Dance. He is also a member of the Publications Committee for the American Association of Physical Activity and Recreation. Doug achieved his master's degree in park and recreation administration from the University of Illinois in 1999 and was appointed director of educational sales for Sagamore Publishing that same year. Sanders has served as editor of the *Management Strategy* newsletter; marketing manager for the *Journal of Park and Recreation Administration* and *Human Dimensions of Wildlife*; and is the originator of the electronic newsletter *SagamoreNet*. Additionally, Sanders has several years of field experience through local park and recreation agencies as an assistant youth sports coordinator at the Champaign County YMCA, Lake House manager at the Urbana Park District, and continues as a nationally certified umpire.

Meredith Bridgers, CPRP

Meredith Bridgers is currently the senior manager of information resources for the National Recreation and Park Association(NRPA). Her work at NRPA encompasses a variety of information services including research, technical assistance, publication, and the Joseph Lee Memorial Library and Archives. She also has over 13 years of experience in the park and recreation field working with federal, state, and local government agencies. Meredith is a graduate of the recreation management program of East Carolina University and Arizona State University.

PREFACE

In 1987 and 1989, the National Recreation Foundation made grants to the National Recreation and Park Association to establish a Recreation and Park Hall of Fame to posthumously honor individuals who had made outstanding and lasting contributions to the park and recreation movement.

Concern had been expressed by the late Robert Crawford and others that the younger generation of both citizens and professional leaders had little knowledge of the enormous struggles and extraordinary contributions of some of the early pioneers in this field.

The Hall of Fame was brought to fruition by a group of leaders in both the American Academy for Park and Recreation Administration and the National Recreation and Park Association. The first group of early leaders were inducted in the Recreation and Park Hall of Fame in 1988 at the National Recreation and Park Congress held in Indianapolis, Indiana.

Profiles in Leadership provides individuals biographies of the 34 men and women who have been elected to date to the Hall of Fame. The book provides a remarkable history of the public recreation and park movement in America. It is an essay on some of the forgotten giants in this field who have paved the way for today's leaders. Their stories are an inspiration to us all.

All proceeds from the sale of *Profiles in Leadership* are to be placed in a restricted fund for use on future Hall of Fame projects.

Lois G. Finkleman, Chair
National Recreation and
Park Association

Chuck Wilt, President
American Academy for Park and
Recreation Administration

ACKNOWLEDGEMENTS

The editors would like to acknowledge the principle sources of information on individuals included in *Profiles in Leadership*. The late George D. Butler's book, *Pioneers in Public Recreation*, was used extensively for material on early recreation pioneers, particularly those affiliated with the National Recreation Association. John L. Crompton's recent book, *Twentieth Century Champions of Parks and Recreation*, provided a wealth of information on early park leaders. Autobiographies written by Conrad L. Wirth, Thomas E. Rivers, Lemuel A. Garrison, and Robert W. Crawford were very useful in providing information on their careers. Hilmi Ibrahim's, *Pioneers in Leisure and Recreation*, was helpful in providing data on George D. Butler, Thomas E. Rivers, and Robert W. Crawford.

Major gratitude is due to the following individuals who have served as members of the Hall of Fame Selection Committee over the past 20 years.

Past Hall of Fame Selection Committee Members:

Charles E. Hartsoe, Ph.D.
Anne S. Close
Joseph J. Bannon, Ph.D.
Robert W. Crawford
Tony Mobley, Ed.D.
R. Dean Tice
Robert F. Toalson
Donald Henkel, Ph.D.

Beverly D. Brandes
H. Douglas Sessoms, Ph.D.
Ira Hutchinson
Michelle Park
Jodi A. Landry
Kathryn Poster
Van Anderson, Ph.D.
Lee Furr

A special word of thanks is due to Sagamore Publishing and Joseph J. Bannon. Special gratitude is also due to Jose Barrientos, production coordinator and book designer, for his splendid cooperation and talent. We also express our appreciation to Lisa Sanders, Hilary Sullenberger, Jim Voight, and Joyce Hartsoe for their editorial assistance in the production of this book.

SPONSORS

National Recreation and Park Association
www.nrpa.org

The National Recreation and Park Association (NRPA) is a non-profit service, research, and education organization, representing the united voice of the park and recreation movement. For over 100 years, the organizations that make up NRPA have been dedicated to the positive use of leisure time, conservation of our natural and human resources, and beautification of the American movement. The Association serves federal, state, and local governments as well as private organizations and citizen efforts.

NRPA embodies the heritage of the American Instititute of Park Executive (1898), the National Recreation Association (1906), the National Conference on State Parks (1921), and the American Recreation Society (1937). This unification was acconplished by amending the charter of the National Recreation Association.

American Academy of Park and Recreation Administration
www.aapra.org

The American Academy for Park and Recreation Administration (AAPRA), established in 1980, is a non-profit organization of distinguished practitioners and scholars committed to the advancement of park and recreation administration. The Academy encourages scholarly efforts by both practitioners and educators to develop and enhance the practice of administration in the park, recreation, and leisure service fields.

BENEFACTOR

National Recreation Foundation
www.nationalrecreationfoundation.org

The National Recreation Foundation (NRF) is a nonprofit charitable foundation administered by a citizens' Board of Trustees. The Foundation was started to initiate and support the promotion and development of leadership, programs, and facilities in the field of recreation and parks.

Since 1919, members of the Foundation's Board of Trustees historically have represented diverse areas of the United States and different facets of American life. They have always shared three common bonds: a love of recreation, a deep respect for its value in all our lives, and the belief that high quality recreation programs are vital in fostering social stability in our communities.

The Foundation supports aggressive campaigns to increase the fitness level of all Americans. The NRF considers this particularly important in view of the ever escalating cost of health care in the United States. Priority is given to cooperative, coordinated efforts among local, state, and national agencies that address the reduction of health care costs through prevention. Recreation and park organizations are encouraged to develop responses to the societal problem of maintaining a healthy lifestyle. It is well documented that recreation participation results in healthier living, which helps alleviate the cost of health care.

INTRODUCTION

The public recreation and park movement in America is an outgrowth of the urbanization that occurred in the 19th and 20th centuries. It owes its existence and growth to the vision and dedication of individuals who have worked to improve the quality of life in America through parks and recreation. Many of these leaders made extraordinary contributions, yet have been virtually forgotten in today's hectic society.

There was some concern about the proliferation of recognition programs for individuals who have made contributions to the park and recreation movement. The giants of the park and recreation field over the years had been ignored and perhaps too much attention was being given to contemporary, possibly short-lived, contributions. The late Robert W. Crawford suggested the possibility of creating a "Public Recreation and Park Hall of Fame" to honor those who have made extraordinary contributions to the park and recreation field.

With a special grant from the National Recreation Foundation, a Recreation and Park Hall of Fame was established and named in honor of Robert W. Crawford. Crawford was one of the most important leaders in the recreation and park field at the turn of the 20th century.

From its inception, the Hall of Fame has been a joint venture between the American Academy for Park and Recreation Administration (AAPRA) and the National Recreation and Park Association (NRPA). The Hall of Fame is located in the Ahrens Institute at the NRPA headquarters in Ashburn, VA, where commemorative plaques are displayed and available for viewing by the public. Additional information about the Hall of Fame is available in the Joseph Lee Memorial Library and Archives as well as on the NRPA website. While the Hall of Fame is a memorial to those leaders in the park and recreation movement who have enriched our philosophy and enhanced our environment, it is hoped that recognizing the accomplishments of selected early leaders will serve as an inspiration for future leaders.

Our society is rapidly changing, both old and new issues cry out for leadership: increased urbanization, a newly-defined youth culture, expanded immigration from South America and Asian cultures, urgent environmental problems, and concern for public health are just a few.

Recreation and parks have much to contribute to a healthy, happy, and cohesive society. Understanding the past and the role that individual leaders played is essential to understanding the present and for planning intelligently for the future.

Charlie E. Hartsoe
M. Douglas Sanders
Meredith Bridgers

" Life is best enjoyed when time periods are evenly divided between labor, sleep, and recreation...all people should spend one-third of their time in recreation which is rebuilding, voluntary activity, never idleness. "

– Brigham Young

SELECTION CRITERIA

Robert W. Crawford
Recreation and Park Hall of Fame
www.nrpa.org/halloffame

The Recreation and Park Hall of Fame recognizes individuals who have made outstanding and lasting contributions to the advancement of recreation and parks in the United States. The Hall of Fame is jointly sponsored by the National Recreation and Park Association and the American Academy of Park and Recreation Administration, with the support of the National Recreation Foundation.

To be selected, a nominee must meet the following criteria:

- Have made an outstanding and lasting contribution to the advancement of the park and recreation movement in the United States.

- The contributions must have been made in relationship to the mission of the National Recreation and Park Association and its parent organizations.

- Selection to the Hall of Fame is a posthumous honor. No nominee shall be considered until at least five years following death.

- Nominees will be considered for their contributions to the recreation and park field warranted by historical review and evaluation of long-term impact upon the recreation and park movement without regard to race, sex, religion, or age.

The Hall of Fame, is open to the public and special commemorative plaques are on display at the National Recreation and Park Association headquarters in Virginia.

To nominate an individual visit www.nrpa.org/halloffame. Inductions are held at NRPA's Annual National Congress and Exposition.

ROBERT W. CRAWFORD
RECREATION AND PARK
HALL OF FAME

INDUCTEES
1988 - 2005

Inducted October 1989

> *"It is as if our cities had not yet developed a sense of responsibility in regard to the life of the streets, and continually forget that recreation is stronger than vice, and that recreation alone can stifle the lust for vice. "*
>
> *–Jane Addams*

Jane Addams
1860 - 1935

Born in Cedarville, IL, Laura Jane Addams was the daughter of John and Sarah Addams. John Addams, a prominent businessman, was president of the local bank, owner of two mills, a member of the Illinois Assembly, and friend and colleague of Abraham Lincoln. Due to her mother's death, Addams' father instilled upon her the values of philanthropy and caring for the citizens of their community at an early age. Upon her father's encouragement to pursue a higher education, Addams enrolled at nearby Rockford Female Seminary from 1877-1881, where she developed an interest in philosophical, economic, and social issues. After graduation, Addams traveled abroad to Europe. While touring England she was introduced to Toynbee Hall, a settlement house in the slums of London. This experience marked the beginning of her calling to the social work profession.

Within a few years of returning to the United States, Jane Addams and her travel companion, Ellen Gates Starr, committed themselves to the idea of starting a settlement house in Chicago. On September 18, 1889,

Hull House, Chicago, 1898
The New England, July 1898

Hull House was founded to offer social services targeted towards the urban poor. At its height, approximately two thousand individuals visited Hull House weekly. Its facilities and staff of volunteers provided disadvantaged families with social services and activities in one central location. This included programs such as medical treatment, childcare, temporary shelter, and legal aid. Hull House also provided classes for immigrants to learn English, vocational skills, music, art and drama—a forerunner of the continuing education classes offered by today's community colleges.

Jane Addams entered the recreation field in 1893 when she acquired a nearby building to Hull House and transformed it into a coffee house and gymnasium. She also obtained a nearby housing slum and converted it into a playground. Addams was in the forefront of a national movement promoting the importance of organized play in urban environments. Demonstrating that recreation served as an ideal training ground for democratic citizenship, she stressed that recreation was more than sport and physical education; it was the source of creativity. In 1906, Jane Addams was one of the founding members of the Playground Association of America (PAA) and served as a member of its first Board of Directors.

Her writings, especially her book, *The Spirit of Youth and the City Streets,* alerted the American people to the significance of recreation as a basic human necessity. She was elected second vice-president of the PAA at its organization meeting and took a vital interest in the recreation movement. Her conviction that recreation and social work were closely interrelated was clearly revealed in her speech, "Recreation and Social Morality" at the Play Congress in 1907.

In addition to Hull House and the recreation movement, Jane Addams was a leader in the plight for women and the

Jane Addams, 1912
Public Domain, Library of Congress

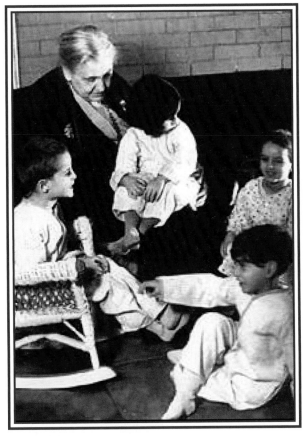

Jane Addams never lost her concern and devotion for children.
University of Illinois, Chicago

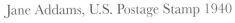

Jane Addams, U.S. Postage Stamp 1940

peace movement. In 1915, in an effort to avert World War I, Jane Addams organized the Women's Peace Party and the International Congress of Women. In 1919 she was elected first president of the Women's International League for Peace and Freedom, a position she held until her death. She was a founding member of the American Civil Liberties Union (ACLU). She was a charter member of the National Association for the Advancement of Colored People (NAACP), having answered the "call" in 1909 that led to the organization's formation.

When the depression of the 1930's struck, Addams saw many of the things she had advocated and fought for become policies under President Franklin Roosevelt. In recognition of her work for world peace, she was awarded the Nobel Peace Prize in 1931, becoming the first American woman to receive this honor. Jane Addams was one of the nation's most influential advocates for social issues of her time. It was no accident that a woman such as her should share in the building of the recreation movement–a movement for a more abundant life.

Adapted from:

Addams, J. (1909). *The spirit of youth and the city streets.* New York: The Macmillan Company.

Addams, J. (1910). *Twenty years at Hull-House.* New York: The Macmillan Company.

Braucher, H. (June 1935). Jane Addams, *Recreation.* 135.

Butler, G.D. (1965). *Pioneers in public recreation.* Minneapolis, MN: Burgess Publishing Company.

Hartsoe, C. (2007). *Building better communities*: *The story of the National Recreation Association (1906-1965).* Champaign, IL: Sagamore Publishing.

Ibrahim, H. (1989). *Pioneers in leisure and recreation.* Reston, VA: American Alliance for Health, Physical Education, Recreation, and Dance.

The welfare of any segment of a community should be a concern of all.

–Ernest T. Attwell

Inducted October 1989

Ernest T. Attwell
1878 - 1949

Ernest T. Attwell, affectionately known as "E.T." to countless friends and colleagues, was born in New York City. His mother was a leader in social and charitable affairs. His father was rector of St. Philip's Protestant Episcopal Church, one of the largest and oldest churches in Harlem, NY. Following his early education in New York City and Brooklyn, Attwell worked eight years in the office of the Southern Pacific Railroad Company, where he gained experience in business methods and management, which proved to be valuable throughout his life.

At the turn of the century, Attwell joined the staff at Tuskegee Institute, AL, where he was a close associate of Booker T. Washington. He was in charge of the Institute's business department, coached football, and took a close personal interest in the students' recreation. During the last 12 years at the Institute, Attwell served as a member of the faculty and of the executive council of the governing body. He was also responsible for extension work in cooperation with the Alabama State Business League, of which he was president for several years.

The Attwell Story, Cover
National Recreation Association, 1951

During World War I, Attwell served as assistant to the food administrator for the State of Alabama. His knowledge for organization soon caught the attention of the Honorable Herbert Hoover, who called him to Washington to assist the U.S. Food Administration on the regulation of nation-wide work among African-American people in the wartime conservation of food. By this time, Attwell's perceptive and statesmanship in the field of interracial wellbeing had been noted by the National Recreation Association (NRA), and at the request of the Association joined its staff in March 1919.

In July 1920, Attwell became field director of the Association's Bureau of Colored Work, a title he held until his death in 1949. At the time, few cities provided recreation programs for African-Americans; in fact, such programs first emanated largely from centers established for military personnel by the War Camp Community Service. His first assignment was to transform these centers into permanent peacetime operations in 27 communities. His work required tact in dealing with organizational problems in such cities as Philadelphia, Montgomery, and Mobile. During the first nine years after he joined the Association's staff, the number of cities reporting African-American leaders to the *Recreation Yearbook* increased from 28 to 103, and the number of such leaders from 35 to over 400. A few years later the Bureau of Colored Work reported: "There are at least a hundred communities

Egyptian pageant presented by African-American children at Mosely Recreation Center, Chicago 1926.
Library of Congress, American Memory Collection

developed during the past decade, which have as a part of their recreation program some organized recreation unit for colored people, which did not exist before."

In visiting communities which have approached the recreation frontier in tolerant and considerate spirit, I find not so much a difference in the technical direction of wholesome recreation activities for colored people, as a difference in the problems to be faced in promoting available facilities and leadership. That these problems have been recognized and in many ways adjusted is indicated in the unusual growth of the available centers and playgrounds for colored groups in every section of the United States.

–Ernest Attwell

More than 100 African-American children took part in the fairy pageant "The Magic Path," on the campus of Virginia Union University by the Colored Playground and Recreation Association of Richmond, VA.
Library of Congress, American Memory Collection

The recruitment, training, and effective placement of qualified recreation leaders of his race ranked high among Attwell's

An annual city-wide contest in radio construction at Douglas Playground, Chicago.
Library of Congress, American Memory Collection

objectives and achievements. Much of his time was devoted to improving the quality of recreation leaders and to enlisting promising young people for service in this field. For many years the conduct of five-week schools for the training of leaders in recreation philosophy and techniques was a major feature of his yearly schedule. Held in various cities around the country, conducted by a staff from the National Recreation School, and directed by Attwell, the schools offered a comprehensive, intensive course at a minimum fee. They served a valuable purpose, because few college courses were then available, and the number of trained African-American recreation leaders was very small.

When President Coolidge called his famous National Conference on Outdoor Recreation, Attwell was invited as a delegate. From the 150 organizations represented, 60 delegates were selected as the Executive Council of the Conference. Attwell was selected to serve on this Council. Later, he also served as a member of President Hoover's Conference on Child Health and Protection.

Attwell devoted his time and energy to the park and recreation movement It was because of his vision participants are treated

National Community Recreation School for African Americans, Chicago, IL, 1925. Ernest Attwell pictured second from the right on the front row.
Colors of Recreation 1996 NRPA and Ethnic Minority Society and from Archives

Two years ago a friend asked me what I new about Ernest T. Attwell. I responded, "Very little." He suggested I learn more about Attwell. In doing further research, I was amazed to find information on a remarkable American who made a lasting contribution in developing recreation opportunities for minority groups.

Attwell spent 12 years at Tuskegee Institute where he was an associate of Booker T. Washington. In 1919, he joined the staff of the National Recreation Association where he headed the Bureau of Colored Work. For over 30 years, Earnest T. Attwell worked to expand recreation opportunities, facilities, and leadership for African-American citizens in scores of communities across the nation.

In various tributes he was called one of the truly great men of his generation, a pioneer in the field of enhancing a more abundant life, and a man who left his imprint on hundreds of communities throughout the country.

Joseph Wynns, CPRP
Director, Indy Parks and Recreation
Past President, American Academy for Park and Recreation Administration

A good recreation program requires good leadership, and toward the end that this may be provided, recreation training courses and conferences were held. The above area conference in St. Louis, MO, was one of the last at which Attwell presided. Joining Attwell were members of his staff, Grace Walker directly behind him, and James Madison, in the front row third from right. Attwell may be seen at the extreme right, third row back, while young Attwell II, is in the immediate foreground.
The Attwell Story

equal without regard to race or social position. He was called "One of the truly great men of his generation, a pioneer in the field of providing a more abundant life, an inspiration to workers in the recreation profession, and a man who left an indelible imprint upon hundreds of communities across the country." Attwell accomplished more than any other individual in securing quality recreation opportunities for minority groups in this country.

Adapted from:

Attwell, E.T. (August, 1926). Recreation for colored America, *The American City Magazine*. 162-165.
Butler, G.D. (1965). *Pioneers in public recreation*. Minneapolis, MN: Burgess Publishing Company.
Hartsoe, C. (2007). *Building better communities: The story of the National Recreation Association (1906-1965)*. Champaign, IL: Sagamore Publishing.
National Recreation Association (September, 1949). Ernest Ten Eyck Attwell, *Recreation*. 307-309.
National Recreation Association (1951). *The Attwell story*. Ashburn, VA:

Inducted October 2003

"The elderly need economic security, adequate health services at reasonable cost, and challenges that give them a sense of the worth of living."

–Edith L. Ball

Edith L. Ball
1905-1996

Originally from New York City, Edith Ball earned her Bachelor of Science degree in health and physical education and a Master of Arts degree in higher education from Columbia University. Her professional career began in 1925 as a Girls Club Leader for the York Settlement House in New York. For the next 25 years Ball served with distinction in many leadership positions while teaching health and physical education classes at Kent State College, Columbia University, and the University of Maryland. In the early part of the 1930s, Ball was appointed

director of physical education and recreation in the Western Reserve School of Nursing. For the next six years she taught classes and developed recreation programs for students, hospital staff, and patients. Out of this experience, therapeutic recreation became an interest and she began using recreation as motivation for giving patients a will to live.

From 1937 to 1943, Ball was employed by the Works Projects Administration where she served as supervisor of recreation, district director of communities,

American Recreation Society Officers, 1961: From Left: Graham Skea, Assistant Treasurer; Stewart G. Case, Second Vice President; William Frederickson Jr., President; Edward H. Thacker, First Vice President; Edith Ball, President-Elect; Henry T. Swan, Secretary; and Louis Twardzik, Treasurer. Officers were installed at the 43rd National Recreation Congress, Detroit, MI.
American Recreation Journal, October 1961

and director of War Service Activities for Maryland, DE, and the District of Columbia. Among her numerous responsibilities was organizing community recreation services in 23 Maryland counties, developing specialized programs for pre-school children, and developing recreation services in hospitals and homes. The belief of recreation as a therapeutic tool in working with these populations helped to advance her programming efforts and lead to her involvement in the organization of recreation activities and services for military personnel.

Ball was appointed in 1943 as assistant director and then director of recreation and education for the Office of Residence Halls, Washington, D.C. She was responsible for the organization and operation of programs in four recreation buildings and 18 residences for 11,000 women government workers and their friends. In 1947, she left the federal government to become the executive director of Stuyvesant Neighborhood House in New York City, a position she held until 1950. At Stuyvesant House, she

directed the operation of a full settlement house program for 1,500 members and the operation of a summer residential camp. She also began a doctoral studies program in recreation administration at New York University, which she completed in 1953.

For the next 23 years, Ball served as instructor, assistant associate, full professor, and chairman in the School of Education at New York University. Through her teaching and providing leadership and direction to the program in the areas of recreation

During the period 1956-1962, Edith Ball served, in succession as Chair of the Hospital Section, Secretary, Second Vice President, First Vice President, President Elect, and President of the American Recreation Society.

Edith Ball presides at the annual American Recreation Society Awards and Citations Luncheon, 45th National Recreation Congress, St. Louis, MO.
American Recreation Journal, November-December 1963

leadership, administration, and hospital recreation, Ball created the precursor to what is now known as therapeutic recreation. In 1973, when she retired, Ball was appointed professor emerita. She continued to teach as an adjunct professor at both New York University and George Washington University, until 1975 when she moved to Tucson, AZ. While in Tucson, she taught courses at the University of Arizona and Texas Woman's University, served as a member and chair of the Therapeutic Recreation Advisory Council for the City of Tucson Parks and Recreation Department and was active in the state society.

Throughout her professional career, Ball was active in local, state, and national organizations. From 1937, when she served for three years as chair of the Division of Girl's and Women's Sports for the Maryland State Association of Health, Physical Education, and Recreation, until 1994, she was involved as an officer or committee chair in numerous organizations. During the period 1956-1962 she served, in succession as chair of the Hospital Section, secretary,

second vice president, first vice president, president elect, and president of the American Recreation Society. From 1962-1965, Ball served on the national committee, which brought together eight organizations to form the National Recreation and Park Association (NRPA). After the merger, she served on the Board of Trustees from 1965 through 1973. During this period she was also a member of the Boards of Directors of the Society of Park and Recreation Educators (SPRE) and of the National Therapeutic Recreation Society (NTRS). She was appointed as chair of the National Accrediting Committee of SPRE in 1967 and was instrumental in the development of the Council on Accreditation formed by NRPA and the American Association for Recreation and Leisure in 1976. She served as chair or member of the Council for several years. In 1970, she became a founding member of the Scholarship Committee of the World Leisure and Recreation Association (WLRA) and remained an active member until 1996.

Accreditation Project Committee-From Left seated: Gordon Starr, Dr. Betty van der Smissen, Shirley Gaillard, Jean Sanford, Dr. Janet Maclean, Anne Bushart, Dr. Edith Ball, Walter Cook, Dr. Fred Coombs, Dr. Jackson Anderson, Dr. Clifton Hutchins, and Loren Kottner. From Left standing: Dr. Douglass Sessoms, William Kloppe, Frances Cleary, Dr. Martin Meyer, Phyllis Lee, Harold Schrage, and Willard Sutherland. *American Recreation Journal*, March-April 1965

A number of prestigious awards, citations and honors were bestowed upon Ball. Among the most notable are: the SPRE Distinguished Fellow Award (1971); the NTRS Distinguished Service Award (1974); the American Association of Leisure and Recreation J.B. Nash Scholar Lecturer (1979); and the Ernest O. Melby Award for Distinguished Service in Human Relations (1980) by the Alumni Association of the School of Education, New York University. In 1980, Ball became a Charter Fellow in the Academy of Leisure Sciences and in 1981, a Charter Fellow of the Academy of Parks and Recreation Administration. She was made a Life Trustee of NRPA in 1993 and was the recipient of the Ralph C. Wilson Award, established by the Board of Trustees of NRPA and awarded each year to the person who best exemplifies leadership and commitment to the Association. Upon her retirement in 1972, the School of Education Program in Recreation and Leisure Studies at New York University established the Edith Ball Therapeutic Recreation Fund.

Ball was highly respected among her peers. Tony A. Mobley, Dean of the School of Health, Physical Education and Recreation, Indiana University commented, "Dr. Edith Ball was one of the giants in the recreation, parks, and leisure services movement. Always scholarly and challenging in her approach to professional issues, students, and colleagues, she inspired everyone to reach out to 'do their best.' She was always extraordinarily gracious and sensitive to other people. She was a consummate professional and a great lady."

Adapted from:

Academy of Leisure Sciences (October, 1995). *The Academy of Leisure Science celebrates its fifteenth anniversary.*

American Academy of Park and Recreation Administration. (1993). *21st Century management.* Champaign, IL: Sagamore Publishing.

American Academy of Park and Recreation Administration. (1983). *Legends of the American Park and Recreation Association.* Downloaded on May 22, 2008 from http://www.aapra.org/legend.html

National Recreation and Park Association (May, 1997). In memoriam: Dr. Ball remembered, *Parks & Recreation.* 94-98.

Inducted October 1988

"Recreation is not only for the time. Recreation is forever afterward. Each person has his memory chest."

–Howard S. Braucher

Howard S. Braucher
1881-1949

Described as a philosopher, crusader, promoter, and interpreter, Howard Braucher is among the leading pioneers in the recreation movement. Originally from Royalton, NY, he received a Bachelor of Arts degree from Cornell University. While a student, Braucher served as president of the Christian Association and worked at the Church of the Covenant and the Madison Square Church House. His professional career started in 1906 as secretary of Associated Charities in Portland, ME. During this time, his interest in recreation was stimulated as a result of his volunteer service in Portland's evening recreation centers and by a visit he made to a number of cities to study the new recreation movement. From 1909, when he became the first full-time secretary of the Playground Association of America, until his death in 1949, Braucher spearheaded a nationwide movement to bring recreation opportunities to all people, regardless of age, sex, race, or religious faith.

Boardwalk leap frog in Atlantic City, NJ – National Recreation Association (NRA) Secretary Howard Braucher leaps over NRA President Joseph Lee during the 22nd National Recreation Congress.
National Recreation and Park Association Archives

As the guiding force behind the National Recreation Association for 40 years, Braucher believed it was local government's responsibility to provide basic recreation services to the general public. During this time, community recreation in the United States won wide support. Funding for local recreation programs increased phenomenally in the first half of the twentieth century, from one million in 1909 to 96 million in 1948. Much of the growth of public recreation is attributed to Braucher and the efforts of the National Recreation Association.

At the onset of World War I, Braucher, along with Joseph Lee, was instrumental in organizing the War Camp Community Service (WCCS) to provide off-base recreation opportunities for military personnel. Under their direction, WCCS established clubhouses in towns and cities near military bases and employed a staff of 2,500, who were assisted by 60,000 volunteers. This wartime community service helped to stimulate the expansion of public recreation during the 1920s.

WCCS poster from World War I
Playground and Recreation Association of America

Among his other pioneering efforts, were the establishment of a National Physical Education Service and the creation of the National Recreation School. The National Physical Education Service, implemented in the 1920s, represented a nationwide campaign to make physical education compulsory in elementary and secondary schools. The National Recreation School, established in New York City in 1926, provided a one-year graduate program to train men and women to serve as recreation executives in cities across the country. Both of these institutions provided early on a set of standards and trained professionals for communities.

The importance of Braucher is evident in his writing in the monthly magazine known as *Recreation*, formerly called *The Playground* and later *Playground and Recreation*. For many years, *Recreation* magazine carried on its editorial page Braucher's wise and timely comments on the ways of the world, with particular reference to the field of recreation. When unemployment was a major problem in the United States, he called on recreation to meet the challenge of empty hours and emptier pockets. When dictatorship enveloped half of Europe, no one realized more clearly than he how easily organized recreation could be made an instrument for enslaving the souls of men. He saw what "Strength through Joy"[1] had come to mean in Germany and he was unwavering in his determination that no such corruption of the spirit of recreation should come to pass in America. When war was declared, he was among the first to affirm that service to country must come first, that play must wait for the leisure moments when all work was done; but he never ceased to emphasize the importance of play as a builder of morale and a source of strength for continued effort.

Heckscher Foundation Building where the National Recreation School was located.
National Recreation and Park Association Archives

[1] "Strength through Joy" was a state-controlled leisure organization in the Third Reich, a part of the German Labour Front. The organization's goal was to create a "people's community" through organized and structured recreation programs.

The World at Play

PLAY is a universal language. In the kingdom, or republic if you will, of play there are no boundaries except those that separate the living from the dead; those who still play from those who do not.

In every country play and recreation will have a vital part in shaping the new culture, the new art, the new life of man.

In all lands leisure increases—even though the rate of increase is greater in some countries than in others. Art, music, drama, sport, adventure are central to leisure. Play and recreation cannot lightly be tossed aside by those who care what kind of world their children's children shall live in.

As we understand one another's play and recreation; as we share more fully knowledge of what we really want to do when we are under no compulsion; as we know how we are alike and how we are different in our deepest desires, what we really are when we are ourselves, —then we shall be better able to live together in a world that each year is made smaller by radio and airships. Progress lies not in making each nation's play alike, but in giving opportunity for all individuals, groups and nations from out of all the infinite possibilities of growth and development to become what will give the most permanent and enduring satisfaction.

The play tradition of the United States owes much to Germany, to England, and to other countries—yet after all it is essentially American. In the field of play and recreation there must never be tariff walls.

HOWARD BRAUCHER.

"The pioneering spirit is leading us in the recreation movement to the discovery of a vast continent of human values hitherto unsuspected, richer treasures, richer in real values than all the geographical continents of the world put together."

L. P. Jacks, LL.D.

413

Editorial page from *Recreation*, October 1931.

THE WHITE HOUSE
WASHINGTON

July 16, 1942

Dear Mr. Braucher:

The stated purpose of the War Recreation Congress - to mobilize the recreation forces of the nation for more effective war service - is an admirable one. I earnestly hope it will be successful.

The inventive genius and organizing power of our people gave us the economic freedom that made possible the wide-spread development of recreation for all the people. Now that we are at war we are fortunate in having this rich resource of recreation to give us physical, mental and spiritual power for the titanic task at hand. You who have devoted your lives to this movement well know that unless its full resources are geared to the war effort till victory comes, all that you hold dear may be lost for generations.

I rejoice in the fact that the strength of the recreation movement in America stems from a deep feeling of community responsibility, and I am greatly encouraged by the reports received of what communities are doing through their local governments and voluntary community committees.

The recreation services being provided for the armed forces, for the workers in war industries, and for the morale of civilian groups are very definitely contributing to our war effort.

As a long time member and supporter of the National Recreation Association, I am happy in the thought of the significant war recreation service being rendered through this great cooperative effort.

Very sincerely yours,

Mr. Howard Braucher,
President,
National Recreation Association,
315 Fourth Avenue,
New York, N. Y.

Franklin D. Roosevelt

National Recreation Association's Archives

At the end of the war, he wrote of the need to establish a sense of brotherhood in the community, in the nation, and in the world, and of recreation as a means to this end. At the time of his death, his editorials, rich in philosophy, were published by the Association in a volume entitled *A Treasury of Living.* They were published in the hope that others reading his words may be inspired to carry on his legacy.

It is difficult to estimate the influence Braucher has had on the growth of community recreation. Braucher preached the gospel of play as an essential part of life. To him, life without recreation was a living death and the man who lacked the spirit of play was an empty shell. His contributions will have lasting value, not only for recreation professionals, but everyone involved in the well being of mankind. One would be hard fast to find a neighborhood that at some time or another has not benefited from the numerous services provided by the National Recreation Association under the leadership of Braucher.

Adapted from:

Butler, G.D. (1965). *Pioneers in public recreation.* Minneapolis, MN: Burgess Publishing Company.

Ibrahim, H. (1989). *Pioneers in leisure and recreation.* Reston, VA: American Alliance for Health, Physical Education, Recreation, and Dance.

Inducted October 1995

"Although it is easy to lose sight of it, the recreation and park profession does not have a role, except what it can do through its efforts to improve the lot of humanity."

–*Charles K. Brightbill*

Charles K. Brightbill
1910-1966

A leader in the recreation and park field from the end of World War II up to the time of his death in 1966, Charles K. Brightbill emerged as one of the leading philosophers and statesmen of his time. From a background that included experience at the local and federal levels of government as well as with a national non-profit association, Brightbill culminated his career at the University of Illinois where he developed one of the most respected higher-education programs in the nation.

Brightbill, a native of Reading, PA, graduated with a Bachelor's degree in commerce and finance from Pennsylvania State University. He received a Master's of Business Administration degree from the University of Pennsylvania. While at Penn State, he was selected to be drum major of Penn State's famed Marching Blue Band.

He began his recreation career while in college working as a picnic specialist for the Reading Department of Playgrounds and Recreation. His last summer in this job, he conducted picnic programs for 54

The Challenge of Leisure was one of Brightbill's last publications before his death in 1966.

organizations, including churches, civic clubs, lodges, and social organizations. His success in this position lead to his appointment to a full-time position of supervisor of special activities for the Reading Department of Recreation.

In 1935, Brightbill accepted a position as head of a new Work Project Administration supported by the Recreation Department in Decatur, IL. Here, he developed the Decatur program into one of the best in the nation for a city of its size. The Decatur program became the subject of a film, "Playtown, U.S.A," produced by the Athletic Institute.

The reputation Brightbill gained in Decatur led to his appointment as New England District Representative of the National Recreation Association. In this assignment, he was responsible for promoting, organizing, and providing technical assistance to New England communities in the establishment and operation of public and private recreation systems.

During World War II, Brightbill worked for the Federal government in a number of defense-related positions, including service as Associate Director of the Recreation division of the Office of Community War Service. He shared the responsibility for overseeing the operations of more than 3,000 U.S. programs and numerous other war recreation services for civilians.

Following the war, he was appointed director of the newly-created Division of Recreation Services of the Veterans Administration. From February 1947 to February

Slipping quietly out of Reading, PA, to carry out his bicycle riding boast, Charles K. Brightbill, one of the department of recreation staff, was the most surprised man on earth when the Eagle's candid camera caught him grinding away on the Princeton road about 18 miles from Reading. Riding with him is Miss Marion A. Shelmerdine, who made him prove he could pedal from Allentown to Reading in less than six hours.
The Reading Eagle, May 1935

1949, he was responsible for the planning, development, and supervision of the VA's growing recreation programs in veteran's hospitals.

In late 1948, President Harry Truman created the Presidential Committee on Religion and Welfare in the Armed Forces. Brightbill served as the first and only executive secretary of this committee. In this capacity, he was responsible for undertaking studies and appraisals of policies and programs related to the workforce of military personnel. Among the studies he directed were Free Time and the Armed Forces, The Military Chaplaincy, and Community Planning for the Peacetime Serviceman.

When the Presidential Committee went out of existence, an unexpected job opportunity came from the University of Illinois to head their fledging Recreation Department in the College of Health, Physical Education, and Recreation. Brightbill, who did not have a doctoral degree, was an attractive candidate because of his national reputation in the recreation field. To recruit Brightbill, the University of Illinois offered him the rank of full professor with immediate tenure. When he accepted, a new course in his career had been determined.

Professor Brightbill adapted readily to the university environment and remarked many times that he wished he had entered university ranks earlier. The University of Illinois position opened the door to the most productive, personally rewarding phase of Brigthbill's entire career.

The success of his work at the University of Illinois is noted in a resolution passed by the Board of Trustees of the National Recreation and Park Association, which states, in part:

As an educator in this field he had few equals. The department which he headed at the University of Illinois has not only been a pioneer in education for leisure, but has turned out men and women with a deep sense of dedication who will make

DEPARTMENT OF RECREATION AND MUNICIPAL PARK ADMINISTRATION

University of Illinois
Champaign, Illinois 61822

August 14, 1964

Mr. James H. Evans
Chairman of the Board
National Recreation Association
8 West Eighth Street
New York, New York 10011

Dear Mr. Evans:

I am writing this from Europe—maybe from this distance my views will be less blurred. I am writing now because in my opinion the merger is a "do-it-now" or "pay-the-penalty" proposition! I say this because the many people who undergird the movement have been knocking at the merger door for a long time. If they cannot get in, they will find other doors to enter.

Frankly, I am amazed that the negotiations for the merger should have come so far only to discover that there is now a maize of conflicting explanations for the "break-down." It is hard to believe the implication that differences in philosophy are only now being unearthed. Of course, communication goes beyond being heard to being understood, and the current barriers may have resulted from such a situation. But if so, the deterrents are not irrevocable, if we move with some haste!

I have a proposal to suggest. It is brief and I hope, clear. It could be subscribed to by all parties this fall in Miami and Houston. Plans for implementation and ironing out the details could come later. It deals with principles and it is these on which early consensus is vital.

This proposal is made upon a few basic assumptions. If they are erroneous, you will only waste your time reading the proposal. I assume:

1. That the AIPE, ARS and NRA, plus a vast majority of their constituents, welcome total, organizational unification.

2. That those involved in the negotiations are persons of integrity and consistency, that they desire unification, and that though they are accountable to their respective policy bodies, the latter have full confidence in them.

3. That unification is essential now, and that anything less than simultaneous consolidation of ARS, NRA and AIPE will dissipate rather than strengthen the forces of unification.

4. That if NRA, AIPE and ARS do not achieve early, organic unification, the movement leadership will become even more fragmentized. Other interests, professions and disciplines will move quickly and ably to the forefront in the field.

5. That the governing board of any democratic institution, in government and out, service agency or fellowship society, may not be self-perpetuating, and must be answerable to its constituency, its supporters—financial and otherwise, its members and the people it purposes to serve.

6. Since service to the layman is the ultimate objective of the new Association, it is reasonable that laymen be in the majority on the top policy board—a practice which is traditional in democracies, at all levels of operation, among non-governmental and governmental groups.

THE PROPOSAL

Purpose: It shall be the primary purpose of the National Recreation and Parks Association to help establish and multiply opportunities for the individual to use his leisure, enforced or otherwise, in ways which will contribute to his full personality development--to focus recreation and park resources upon the betterment of mankind.

This fundamental purpose recognizes the indispensability of competent professional and lay leadership, and firmly commits the Association to developing and advancing the highest professional standards.(*)

Policy Establishing Group: The top, governing board shall consist of laymen and professionals on the basis of 2 to 1, respectively. One third (1/3) of the board, designated here as Item "A," shall be appointed from among laymen now serving on the NRA Board. These appointees shall serve until their successors are appointed, and shall have the power to appoint their successors, ad infinitum. One third (1/3) of the board, designated here as Item "B," shall be chosen by the professionals for definite terms of office, and in a manner to be determined by the professionals. The last one third (1/3) of the board shall be laymen nominated by the professionals, submitting a list of three (3) laymen for each one (1) layman needed. From these nominations, the previously selected two thirds (2/3) of the board, namely, Items "A" and "B," shall elect individuals to bring the board to full membership.

Finance: The new, non-profit Association welcomes and solicits financial support from all sources--laymen, professionals, foundations, business and commerce, including management and labor, and from governmental enterprise, contractually, when such support is appropriate and consistent with the purposes of the Association. These sources will be supplemented by membership fees and charges for services and materials when necessary. The financial structure shall be established in a way as to satisfy the requirements of funds already under the jurisdiction of the several founding organizations, and those which may follow. Moreover, the financial structure and purposes of the new Association shall be such as to make it eligible for tax exemptions currently available in Federal legislation and rulings.

Structural-Organizational Implementation: A sustained effort will be made to establish in each state (and province, if Canada is included) an organizational structure comparable to that described here for the national organization, the powers of the state groups being those not reserved for the national body.

Sincerely,

(Signed) Charles K. Brightbill

Charles K. Brightbill
Head of Department

_____

*Although it is easy to lose sight of it, the recreation and park profession does not have a role, except in terms of what it can do through its efforts to improve the lot of humanity. This is equally true of the American Bar Association, American Medical Association and the National Education Association.

CKB/ja

cc: Ray R. Butler
    Norman Johnson
    Alfred LaGasse
    Joseph Prendergast
    Edward Thacker

Charles Brightbill's National Recreation and Park Association letter of unification to James Evans, Chairman of the Board, National Recreation Association.
National Recreation and Park Association Archives

valuable contributions to this field for years to come. The department is held in high esteem by all those in the field of recreation and parks.

Through his books, writings, and lectures, he was able to record for this and future generations a greater understanding of the challenge of leisure as well as a

Recreation and Municipal Park Faculty and Staff, 1963-1964. Charles Brightbill pictured front row center. Courtesy of University of Illinois, Department of Recreation, Sport, and Tourism.

profound philosophy for the recreation and park profession. He authored or co-authored nine major books and more than 75 published articles.

Brightbill was a strong proponent of the concept of citizen and professional cooperation in the recreation and park field. He developed the principles used in formulating the merger that brought together citizen and professional groups to form the National Recreation and Park Association.

Brightbill's strength of character was ever apparent in his struggle with ill health. In January 1963, after his usual noontime swim, Brightbill fell and it was discovered that his spinal column was fractured. Later in that year, it was determined that he had multiple myeloma, an incurable malignancy of the bone marrow.

He chose not to divulge the terminal nature of his illness to individuals other than his family and one or two close associates. Brightbill wanted to function normally and wished to avoid the sympathy of his professional colleagues. He suffered three additional lumbar fractures prior to his death on August 23, 1966.

The period of his terminal illness proved to be one of the most productive periods of his career. During this time, he continued to teach, write, and participate in professional affairs. He retained his keen sense of humor and refused to permit any discussion of his illness.

The uncomplicated and unassuming nature of Charles K. Brightbill is reflected in his personal assessment of himself:

If he asks what I did for immortality.
I sired a girl and a boy, wrote a book
and planted a tree.

Adapted from:

Brightbill, C. (1963). *The challenge of leisure.* Englewood Cliffs, NJ: Prentice Hall Spectrum Books.

Hartsoe, C. (1970). "The Contributions of Charles K. Brightbill to the Recreation Movement." Unpublished doctoral thesis, University of Illinois; Champaign.

Inducted October 1997

Theresa S. Brungardt
1894-1990

" Recreation is re-creation and that thru play we shall have life and have it more abundantly. "

–Theresa S. Brungardt

Originally from New Jersey, Theresa "Tess" Schmidt Brungardt began her career in recreation in 1917. While still in her teens, she joined the staff of the Playground and Recreation Association of America (PRAA) during the hectic period of World War I. After a time in the headquarters office working as a clerk, she was assigned to Greenville, SC, where she established a successful community recreation program. Later she served for several years as the field secretary for the Association for New England. While in this position, Brungardt gained the confidence and acquaintance of local and state authorities as she assisted them in the development of their recreation programs. Theresa Brungardt's experiences with the Association served as a foundation for a rewarding and successful career in the recreation profession.

Following the Vermont Governor's First State Conference on Recreation in 1943, Governor William H. Wills employed Theresa Brungardt as Vermont's first director of recreation. This appointment was in conjunction with the formation of the Vermont State Recreation Committee. In 1947, this committee evolved through legislative action into the State Board of Recreation. At the time, Vermont was one of two states that had established a Board of Recreation. Brungardt served as the director of the State Board of Recreation from 1947 until her retirement in 1964.

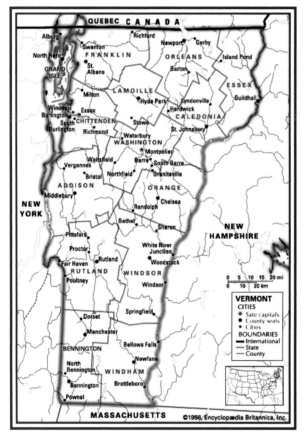

Vermont, the Green Mountain State, is 160 miles long. Its widest northern border is 89 miles while the width at the southern border is 40 ½ miles.

Few guidelines were available to Brungardt as she set about promoting recreation in this rural state. She accepted this as a challenge rather than as a deterrent. Her energy and enthusiasm, combined with her knowledge of recreation through her early work with the PRAA, resulted in remarkable growth in community recreation throughout Vermont. Many small cities throughout the state established recreation departments

under her leadership. Smaller communities were encouraged to provide recreational opportunities through the coordination of volunteer or part-time leaders. The people of Vermont were exposed to the importance of recreation through annual conferences, which Brungardt promoted through her invitation of national recreation leaders as participants. She also provided regional training courses that prepared community leaders for special events. The opportunities for events such as the country-dance helped perpetuate more traditional forms of recreation throughout the state.

An example of the devotion that Brungrardt had in the promotion of recreation at the time was originally published in the *Journal of the American Association for Health, Physical Education, and Recreation.*

One snowy and sleety evening last winter in Vermont, state police were broadcasting warnings to stay off the highways. A little community in the hills, miles from the State House, was expecting the state recreation director to give a talk on recreation, followed by a Valentine's party demonstration. The director telephoned one of the 10 families who lived in the scattered farming community and reported on the dangerous travel conditions. The reply was, "We know it's bad but you can't disappoint us–everyone is coming and the refreshments are all made!"

There was splendid cooperation with all other state departments. A state trooper drove the director over

American Recreation Society "bigwigs" at the White House Conference on Aging huddle with Theresa Brungardt, a member of the national committee for the session. From left: Foster Blaisdell, ARS President; Dr. Harold Meyer, ARS Conference Representative; and ARS Executive Director Howard Jeffrey. *American Recreation Journal*, February 1961

the treacherous roads. The little community had asked for help from the state department of recreation on what to do to keep its young folks in the village Saturday nights. "What can we do except play whist and pitch?" the parents asked. After the program, while everyone enjoyed sandwiches, cake, and coffee, then and there plans were made to have the one-room school lighted every Saturday night. Now, stormy or clear, the young folks have fun in their own community.

According to her colleagues, probably no person has ever worked harder for recreation in Vermont than Brungardt. She was the primary organizer of the Vermont Recreation and Park Association, was actively involved in the work of the Vermont Federation of Women's Clubs, the Vermont Girl Scout Council and president of the Vermont Conference on Social Welfare.

While director of recreation, Brungardt became know nationally for her knowledge, abilities, and experience. National events often invited her to speak, including the White House Conferences on Children and Youth and the White House Conference on the Aging. She served on numerous state and national boards and committees consisting of the National Recreation and Park Association's Board of Trustees, and the National United Service Organizations (USO) Council. Her professional standing was evident by her election as the first female president of the American Recreation Society in 1952, her appointment as recreation chairman of the National Congress of Parents and Teachers, and election as vice-president of the Federation of National Professional Organization for Recreation.

A TRIBUTE TO THERESA S. BRUNGARDT

Stephen E. Baker, Chairman of the Board of Recreation for the State of Vermont, paid the following tribute to Mrs. Theresa S. Brungardt on the occasion of her retirement as Vermont Director of Recreation. "It is my belief that your most remarkable contribution to the citizens of Vermont has been your ability to imprint upon the minds of all of us an awareness of the importance of Recreation, and the constructive use of leisure time. You have impressed us with the idea that Recreation takes its place along with health, education, work and religion as one of the five essentials in every individual's personality and every community's social well-being. You have further impressed upon us that Recreation is closely allied with the fundamental social institutions — the family, church, the school, community, and the state.

You have reminded us frequently that the continuing inclination toward a shorter work week, the progressing stronghold of automation, and an early retirement age, have presented the American public with the problem of what to do with spare time. You have through your efforts convinced the citizens of Vermont that it is wise to invest in Recreation.

Allow me to thank you for the opportunity to work with you, and for the privilege of serving the citizens of Vermont as Chairman of "your" Board. When Governor Stafford originally appointed me, I had no idea that working with you and the Department of Recreation could be such a rewarding experience. Recreation has opened up new vistas in living for me. It has been a means of stimulating interest in those intangible things that bring enrichment and satisfaction so necessary in this great era."

American Recreation Journal, May/June 1964

Free-wheeling participants at the Second Annual Rural Recreation Seminar on Family Recreation in Huntly, IL. From left: George Dow, Richard B. Tomkinson, Theresa S. Brungardt, Reagan B. Brown, John B. Mitchell, and E.A. (Swede) Scholer.
Recreation, October 1963

Few have strived to advance the recreation movement and develop leisure opportunities in communities and small towns as Brungardt. Her involvement in the profession continued even after her retirement in 1964 when she became a board member of the citizen branch of the National Recreation and Park Association. Among the numerous reco-gnitions Brungardt received during her life were the American Recreation Society Fellow Award and Presidential Citation; the Distinguished Professional and Life Member awards of the National Recreation and Park Association; and an honorary Doctor of Humane Letters from Windham College. Since 1974, the Vermont Recreation and Parks Association have paid tribute to her contributions annually with the Theresa S. Brungardt Awards. Brungardt was a genuine pioneer in recreation and many would say a force to be reckoned with in her own right.

Adapted from:

Butler, G.D. (1965). *Pioneers in public recreation*. Minneapolis, MN: Burgess Publishing Company.
National Recreation Association (March, 1964). People in the recreation news, *Recreation*. 147.

Inducted October 1995

"The function of playground administration is to bring to reality the limitless possibilities which the playground affords for fun and good citizenship."

–George D. Butler

George D. Butler
1894-1985

George Butler's legacy to the park and recreation profession has influenced communities throughout the world. He was one of the first to recognize the benefits of parks and recreation in human development. The open space standards he developed in the 1930s guide students, educators, and administrators in the profession to this day. Butler was one of the first instructors of the National Recreation School where he encouraged others to apply these standards in the design and operations of their programs and in their facilities.

Butler came to the National Recreation Association soon after returning from active duty during World War I. An economics major and member of Phi Beta Kappa honor society, Butler earned his degree from Yale University in 1916. His undergraduate studies in French led him to enlist in the military as a section clerk and part-time translator for the United States Ambulance Service, which supported the French Army. For his acts of "courage and endurance," George Butler was awarded the Croix de Guerre Medallion, one of France's highest honors.

Practicing what they preach! Seen at the annual outing for the National Recreation Association headquarters staff, held at Lake Sebago in Palisades Interstate Park. From left: Charles Reed, Field Department; George Butler, Research Department; Joseph Prendergast Executive Director; and Helen Dauncey, Katherine M. Barker Memorial Secretary for Women and Girls.
Recreation, March 1959

In the summer of 1919, Butler returned from military duty to New Haven and his former work with the Yale Bureau of Appointments. Shortly after returning from overseas, he was offered two permanent job positions: one from the National Recreation Association (NRA) and the other from a banking firm, the Guarantee Trust Company. Following his social service calling, Butler signed on as a probationary employee for an annual salary of $1,700 with the NRA. Within two months, Howard Braucher, the NRA's executive secretary, offered Butler a raise and a permanent position as director of research. He accepted and occupied this position for the next 43 years. Soon after Butler joined the Association, the Consultation and Correspondence Bureau was formed as a central clearing house for information and for addressing inquiries. Butler was put in charge and became one of

the most persistent proponents of research in the park and recreation field.

Early in the 20th century there was no park or recreation infrastructure to speak of, no established guidelines for doing things, and no system within which to work. Butler set out to lay an effective foundation for service delivery. First, he articulated the importance of playgrounds for the healthy upbringing of children. Second, he became one of the first instructors in the National Recreation School. Third, he underscored the importance of research to the growth and development of the park and recreation profession. Last and possibly most important, through a series of books ranging from *Playgrounds: Their Administration and Operation* (1936), to *Introduction to Community Recreation* (1940), to *Recreation Areas: Their Design and Equipment* (1947), to *Pioneers in Public Recreation* (1965), Butler catalogued the principles, practices,

George Butler was a founding fellow and member of the Academy of Leisure Sciences (1980).
Recreation, March 1948

At a program honoring volunteers at Bay Village of Sarasota, George Butler was named King of Volunteers for 1981. Volunteers gave from 1,200 to 1,300 hours of service each month in the health center, vesper services, library, and grounds.
Sarasota Herald–Tribune, November 2, 1981

and pioneers that formed the foundation of the contemporary leisure service delivery system. If that was not enough, Butler was assigned to direct three studies of municipal parks in 1930, 1935, and 1940: the first in cooperation with the United States Department of Labor, the second with National Park Service, and the third with the American Institute of Park Executives. These reports provide a picture of the municipal and county park movement at the time which is not available from any other source.

Butler's interests in community affairs were many. He volunteered as a scoutmaster and taught Sunday school at his neighborhood church. He also served as chairman or president for such local groups as the Home-School Association, the Playground Committee, the Board of Adjustment, and the Men's Club. Perhaps the one of which he was most proud was his membership on the Recreation Commission of Leonia, NJ, his hometown. He served the commission from 1946 to 1962. In honor of his contribution, Leonia named its community center gymnasium after him.

George Butler, atop Prospect Mountain, Lake George, NY, August 1970.
Courtesy of Joseph J. Bannon

Butler helped establish the ground floor upon which most all subsequent research, planning, and policy is based in the park and recreation field. The aspects of service that seem so commonplace today exist because Butler had the vision to bring them into fruition. He was a great thinker, a pathfinder, and groundbreaker. His life's work survives by each new research proposal, and his memory will be long cherished. George Butler is not only one of the true pioneers in recreation and parks, he paved the way of research possibilities and changed the direction of the leisure field making it more credible through research.

Adapted from:

Ibrahim, H. (1989). *Pioneers in leisure and recreation.* Reston, VA: American Alliance for Health, Physical Education, Recreation, and Dance.

Dustin, D.L. (October 12, 2004). Making pictures out of clouds: Lessons from the life and times of George D. Butler, *George Butler Lecture Leisure Research Symposium.*

National Recreation Association (February, 1948). At headquarters…George Butler. *Recreation.* 543 & 545.

National Recreation Association (January, 1963). George Butler retires: Forty-three years of service. *Recreation.* 17 & 34.

Recreation is a necessity, not a luxury. It provides an opportunity for re-creation, a chance to make those self-discoveries that lead to fulfillment and happiness.

–Robert W. Crawford

Inducted October 2001

Robert W. Crawford
1906-1995

Born in 1906 to a family of Scottish immigrants, Robert W. Crawford led a life that his sons would later say "epitomized the classic American dream." From coal mining camps to high school and university football fields; as husband, father, and grandfather; from student to teacher; from follower to leader, Crawford rose to the heights of the parks and recreation field and carried a profession with him.

Crawford was a professional in the field of parks and recreation for over 50 years. He graduated from Des Moines University, New York University, and the National Recreation School. Following completion of the 12 month National Recreation School, he accepted a newly created position as director of recreation for the town of Hastings on the Hudson River in New York. His position had been created in response to a local tragedy of one child killing another. Recreation was seen as a means of reducing juvenile delinquency. After six years in Hastings, Crawford accepted a position as director of a new community center at a large public housing project in the Red Hook section of Brooklyn where he stayed for two years.

June 28, 1966, Visitors from Operation Crossroads Africa are greeted by Recreation Commissioner Robert W. Crawford at the dedication ceremonies of the new playground at 16th and Federal Streets.
Philadelphia Department of Recreation

He then became director of recreation for Montclair, NJ, a bedroom community of 50,000 adjacent to New York City. His service here was interrupted by World War II. In February 1944, he accepted a commission in the United States Navy where he would serve as a welfare and recreation officer for the Seventh Fleet in the Philippines.

Following World War II, Crawford was hired as director of recreation in Oakland, CA. After six highly-productive and successful years in Oakland, he was recruited to head a newly reorganized Department of Recreation in Philadelphia, PA. It was here that Robert Crawford enjoyed his greatest accomplishments.

Crawford directed the Philadelphia Recreation Department for more than a quarter of a century. Under his leadership, the city developed one of the finest recreation systems in the country. While serving five mayoral administrations, his department encompassed not only neighborhood parks and playgrounds of the most imaginative and creative design, but included one of the most extensive sport and cultural programs in the nation.

When Crawford came to Philadelphia in 1952 to direct the city's newly organized department of recreation, he took over a program consisting of fewer than 100 facilities. During his 29 year tenure in Philadelphia, he developed the recreation program into one that now has a total of 853 facilities, including 47 recreation centers, 145 playgrounds, 24 park playgrounds, 84 swimming pools, 192 neighborhood parks, 10 play lots, four ice rinks, seven youth camps, and 15 specialty sites including Veteran's Stadium and Kennedy Stadium. He developed a strong relationship with the city's cultural organizations as well as with key business and industry leaders.

National Recreation Association Philadelphia Interns. From left: John Dawson, Betty VanNorman, Robert W. Crawford, John G. Williams, Ralph Laudenshayer, and Charles E. Hartsoe.
Photo compliments of Charles E. Hartsoe

Commissioner Crawford's belief that the community should be involved in decisions affecting their neighborhoods led him to nearly 1,000 public meetings. His commitment to community involvement further led him to establish the Recreation Advisory Council, which grew from seven original members to 3,000 citizen advisors participating in 127 local advisory councils, 12 district councils, and one citywide group. The Philadelphia Department of Recreation became the foremost proponent for citizen participation in the planning, organizing, and developing of community recreation programs.

In addition, while commissioner of recreation, he was elected to serve concurrently as president of the Fairmount Park Commission, a 4,700-acre park within Philadelphia's city limits established in 1867 and managed by a 10 member citizen commission. This honor was symbolic of the confidence that Philadelphia leaders had in Crawford.

Crawford felt a deep responsibility to prepare leaders for the future. While in Philadelphia, he developed a nationally recognized postmasters internship program in cooperation with the National Recreation and Parks Association (NRPA). It trained 42 graduates selected from colleges and universities across the country. He assisted graduates from the program in moving into leadership positions in the recreation and park field throughout the country.

Crawford was nationally recognized as one of the top authorities in the field of recreation and parks. He was the first professional elected to serve as president of the NRPA. He was the recipient of an Honorary Doctor of Public Service degree from Temple University and an Honorary Doctor of Law degree from Grinnell College.

Crawford played a key role in the formation of both the NRPA and the National Recreation Foundation. He

Tennis star Jimmy Connors (third from left) and John McEnroe (second from right), at a tournament in Philadelphia in 1978.

Opera star Luciano Pavarotti (center) posed with Frederic Mann and me after performance in Philadelphia in 1975.

Philadelphia native and Baseball Hall of Fame member Stan Musial, at a ceremony honoring him in 1966.

In 1970, I emceed a luncheon commemorating the 40th anniversary of the Championship fight between Gene Tunney (left) and Jack Dempsey.

Eunice Kennedy Shriver, shown with me at a Philadelphia park in 1968, encouraged us to expand our recreation programming for handicapped children.

Collection of photos from *Reflection of a Recreational Professional*.
National Recreation and Park Association

Veteran's Stadium at the Philadelphia Stadium Complex, managed by the Philadelphia Department of Recreation.
Philadelphia Department of Recreation

The Robert W. Crawford Achievement Prize is awarded annually by the National Recreation Foundation for excellence in leisure to youth.
National Recreation Foundation Annual Review 2005 - 2006

was internationally recognized for his innovative and creative leadership. While he was executive director of the National Recreation Foundation, he was responsible for advancing many new programs around the country. He was also responsible for the creation of many new entities, such as the Recreation and Park Hall of Fame.

Adapted from:

American Academy of Park and Recreation Administration. (1983). *Legends of the American Park and Recreation Association* Downloaded on May 10, 2008 from http://www.aapra.org/legends.html

Crawford, R.W. (1993). *Reflections of a recreation professional*. National Recreation and Park Association.

Ibrahim, H. (1989). *Pioneers in leisure and recreation*. American Alliance for Health, Physical Education, Recreation, and Dance.

Inducted October 1989

Henry S. Curtis
1870 - 1954

Born on a farm in Olivert, MI, Henry Stoddard Curtis attended a local college briefly and went on to graduate from Yale University. In 1898, he received a Ph.D. degree from Clark University in Worcester, MA. At Clark University he studied play activities under the direction of Granville Stanley Hall[1]. After graduation he was appointed director of child studies in the New York City schools and later served as director of school playgrounds. While in New York City, Curtis and Luther Gulick held several meetings to discuss the need for a training course for playground workers. The idea was eventually dismissed with hopes of eventually establishing a national playground association.

In February 1906, Curtis became supervisor of playgrounds in Washington, D.C. He developed the first city-wide

---

[1]Granville Stanley Hall was a psychologist and educator who pioneered American psychology. His interests focused on childhood development and evolutionary theory. Hall was the first president of the American Psychological Association and the first president of Clark University.

Organizers of the Playground Association of America: Beulah Kennard (top left), Dr. George Kober, Commissioner, H. B.F. Macfarland, Walter Hatch, Ellen Spencer Mussey, Charles Weller, Myron T. Scudder, Marie Hofer, Mary McDowell, Amelia Hofer, Dr. Luther H. Gulick, Archibald Hill, Seth T. Steward, Mrs. Samuel Ammon, Sadie American, Dr. Henry S. Curtis (front center), and Dr. Rebecca Stoneroad.
Recreation, Golden Anniversary Issue, June 1956

plan for recreation areas and was a strong advocate for its comprehensive planning. On April 10-15, 1906, he organized the initial meeting, in Washington D.C., which established the Playground Association of America (PAA). Curtis was the Association's first secretary and assistant treasurer, positions he held until 1909. He is also credited for writing the original constitution of the Association.

Curtis played a key role in gaining the public's support and interest in the PAA. He was in charge of organizing their annual congress and publishing its proceedings. At the Jamestown Virginia Congress in 1907, Curtis structured an exhibit in the form of a children's playground. In cooperation with the local schools, programmed play activities were provided. This exhibit, paid for by the Russell Sage Foundation[2], gave thousands of Americans their first view of structured play programs in a playground setting.

Henry Curtis will perhaps be best remembered for his publications for he was a prolific writer during the early years of the recreation movement. He held an exceptional knowledge of the subject and was among the first to realize the importance of providing the recreation field with basic written material. His books *Play and Recreation in the Open Country, Education Through Play, The Practical Conduct of Play, Recreation for Teachers,* and *The Play Movement and Its Significance* were used as college texts and as practical guides for recreation leaders. His frequent contributions to *The Playground* were read primarily by

[2] The Russell Sage Foundation, one of the oldest of America's general purpose foundations, was established in 1907 for "the improvement of social and living conditions in the United States."

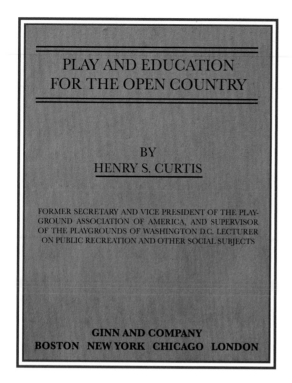

PLAY AND EDUCATION
FOR THE OPEN COUNTRY

BY
HENRY S. CURTIS

FORMER SECRETARY AND VICE PRESIDENT OF THE PLAY-
GROUND ASSOCIATION OF AMERICA, AND SUPERVISOR
OF THE PLAYGROUNDS OF WASHINGTON D.C. LECTURER
ON PUBLIC RECREATION AND OTHER SOCIAL SUBJECTS

GINN AND COMPANY
BOSTON NEW YORK CHICAGO LONDON

RECREATION FOR TEACHERS
OR
THE TEACHER'S LEISURE TIME

BY
HENRY S. CURTIS

New York
THE MACMILLIAN COMPANY 1918
All rights reserved

individuals interested in the movement, but his articles in such journals as the *Annuals of the American Society of Political and Social Science* and *Harper's Monthly* carried the recreation story to a wide public. His pamphlet, *The School Grounds and Their Equipment*, prepared for the Missouri Department of Education, had a wide distribution both inside and outside the state. In all, Curtis published over 90 publications in the recreation field.

Curtis retired in Ann Arbor, MI, where two projects occupied much of his time. One was the promotion of the Huron-Clinton Metropolitan District, which in 1960 comprised six properties with a total of 14,530 acres. He became one of the first to realize the potential recreation value of the Huron and Clinton river valleys while conducting a survey for the University of Michigan. In 1937, Curtis was appointed executive secretary of the Huron-Clinton Parkway Committee, the chief sponsor of the project, which involved the acquisition of a chain of parks and connecting parkways.

Curtis also became an authority on aging issues and persistently supported proposals designed to make the quality of life more enhanced for the elderly. He recommended that large playgrounds have an area to provide leisure opportunities for older adults and suggested they accept some responsibility in assisting playground leaders with programming activities. In addition, he felt games between the elderly and children would rouse much support and interest. It was his intent to make life for the aging more content and meaningful.

Adapted from:

Butler, G.D. (1965). *Pioneers in public recreation.* Minneapolis, MN: Burgess Publishing Company.

Hartsoe, C. (2007). *Building better communities: The story of the National Recreation Association (1906-1965).* Champaign, IL: Sagamore Publishing.

Ibrahim, H. (1989). *Pioneers in leisure and recreation.* Reston, VA: American Alliance for Health, Physical Education, Recreation, and Dance.

Inducted October 1995

"Nobody works all of the time. Everybody plays some of the time. Everybody, in all ages, has played some of the time. A lot of that play, grouped with all sorts of leisure time pursuits, is now called 'recreation.'"

–Charles E. Doell

Charles E. Doell
1894-1983

A native of Minneapolis, MN, Charles Doell spent the majority of his life in the "Land of 10,000 Lakes." In 1916, he graduated from the University of Minnesota, earning a Bachelor of Science degree in civil engineering. Upon graduation, he served with the United States Army Transportation Corps in France at the end of World War I from 1918-1919, attaining the rank of first sergeant. Charles Doell went on to become an articulate and imaginative leader in the national park movement.

Doell started working with the Minneapolis Park Board in 1911 as a part-time draftsman while a student at South High School. After his military service, he rejoined the park staff as an engineer, surveyor, and aide to Theodore Wirth, founder and long-time director of the city's park system. While serving under Superintendent Wirth, Doell played an intricate role in the acquisition and development of land for the Grand Rounds Parkway System, a linking series of park areas in Minneapolis making a circular path around the city.

Doell served as secretary of the Board of the Minneapolis Park Commission for 30 years, during which time he was closely involved both with public politics and expansion of one of the country's most prestigious urban park systems. In 1945, he was named superintendent of the Minneapolis Park Commission, a position he occupied for 14 years with distinction and honor until his retirement in 1959. While superintendent, Doell formed partnerships with the city's schools and churches. Through this unique joint venture, Minneapolis was able to provide adequate land and facilities for their recreation programs.

Known for his congeniality and his genuine interest in people, Doell was widely accepted as a prominent leader. He served as president of the Minneapolis Athletic Club, president of the American Institute of Park Executives, and was a member of the Board of Trustees in the early development of the National Recreation and Park Association. He is also credited as a founding member of the American Academy for Park and Recreation Administration. Toward the end of his career with the Minneapolis Park Commission, Doell worked as a park and recreation consultant. In 1957, upon request of the United States Secretary of the Interior, he served as an expert on a needs assessment survey for the National Capital Parks System in Washington, D.C. In the same year, he participated in similar surveys for the Westchester County Park System in New York and the Tulsa Park System in Oklahoma.

Doell was a great student of park philosophy and history. He wrote several chapters in Lebert Weir's two-volume manual *Parks: A Manual of Municipal and County Parks*. He collaborated with Paul J. Thompson, an attorney, to write the book

American Institute Park Executives

Charles E. Doell

CHARLES E. DOELL of Minneapolis and Paul V. Brown of Indianapolis were recently elected president and vice-president respectively of the American Institute of Park Executives. The annual election of officers and two directors was held on September 24 at the San Francisco Convention.

A member of the Institute for over twenty-five years, Charles Doell started in park work during his school days, in 1911. Working continuously for the Minneapolis Park Department—except for a period of service in the first World War—he progressed from assistant engineer to assistant superintendent and in August 1945 became superintendent. During his long period of Institute membership, Charles Doell has served the organization in several important capacities, has taken part in numerous convention programs and has served on Institute committees.

The new vice-president, Paul V. Brown, was superintendent of state parks in Indiana and assistant director of the Indiana Conservation Department until 1943. He is now director of parks and recreation at Indianapolis.

Earl F. Elliot was reelected to the office of treasurer and George L. Chesley of New Britain, Connecticut, and George I. Simons of Atlanta, Georgia, were elected directors of the Institute for the next three years.

Recreation, December 1947

Founding meeting of the National Recreation and Park Associations Board of Trustees, August 13-14, at the Americana Hotel, New York City. Charles Doell was a founding member of the Board.
National Recreation and Park Association Archives

Public Park Policies and with Gerald Fitzgerald of the University of Minnesota on *Origin and Development of Parks and Recreation* and *A Brief History of Parks and Recreation in the U.S.* As a consistent contributor to *Recreation* magazine and *Parks and Recreation* magazine, he on occasion also contributed to other Canadian and English publications. He was editor of the *Minnesota Engineer*, a publication of the Minnesota Federation of Engineering Societies.

In 1957, Doell was awarded the Cornelius Armory Pugsley Medal "in recognition of his long and distinguished service in the field of municipal parks and recreation and his valuable contributions to the nation at large through his writing, lecturing, and consultations." After retirement, Doell was appointed as a visiting professor of park administration at both Michigan State University and Texas Technological University (1960 to 1966).

While developing and instructing courses at Michigan State University, he wrote the textbook *Elements of Park Administration* (1963). To honor his academic contributions, Michigan State University created the Charles E. Doell Student Leadership Award, which has been presented annually to an undergraduate majoring in park and recreation administration since 1972.

As a national spokesman for the park profession, Doell advocated adamantly for providing quality in public service. He insisted that park professionals should provide both a quality product and quality service within a framework of morality. "This [morality] should be of a high degree and as close to the array of the virtues of a Galahad or a Lancelot as reality will permit in both private and public business. But, it may be observed that while desire for high quality is prevalent in private business, it is essential in public business." Doell's

Minneapolis Park Superintendents Christian Bosen, Charles Doell, and Theodore Wirth, September 15, 1948.
Minneapolis Park System 1883 - 1944. Minneapolis Park Legacy Society

contributions to the park and recreation profession exemplify both quality product and service, and show how persistence in dedication to the field can lead to excellence.

Adapted from:

American Academy of Park and Recreation Administration. (1983). *Legends of the American Park and Recreation Association* Downloaded on May 10, 2008 from http://www.aapra.org/legends.html

Crompton, J.L. (2007). *Twentieth century champions of parks and conservation: The Pugsley award recipients 1928-1964. Volume I.* Champaign, IL: Sagamore Publishing.

Inducted October 1989

" During working hours, we make a living. During leisure hours, we make a life. "

–Dorothy C. Enderis

Dorothy C. Enderis
1880 - 1952

Known as "The Lady of the Lighted Schoolhouse," Dorothy Caroline Enderis was born in Elmhurst, IL, a suburb of Chicago. With the exception of the first year of her life she lived in Milwaukee, WI. her entire life. Upon graduating from high school, Enderis enrolled at Milwaukee Normal School[1], a two-year school for elementary teachers. After completing her degree, she took a summer course in library science and was hired at the Normal School Library, where she worked for eight years.

In 1909, Enderis became a fourth grade teacher in Milwaukee's Fifth Ward School. Know as "The Bloody Fifth," the school was located in a depressed section of Milwaukee's inner city. This position afforded her the opportunity to observe the multicultural dynamics of the community. In 1912, the school board established an extension department which eventually became the Municipal Recreation and Adult Education Department. Enderis was employed by Harold Berg, the initial extension department director, to assist in

---

[1] In 1927, Milwaukee Normal School became Milwaukee State Teachers College offering four-year bachelor's degrees. Both schools were early predecessors of the University of Wisconsin-Milwaukee.

Lighted School House in Milwaukee.
Milwaukee Public Library

the operation of two afterschool centers. In 1920, Enderis was appointed director of the department and expanded their programs into six social centers and 14 playgrounds. By the time she retired in 1948 the department was operating 32 indoor centers, 62 playgrounds, and a variety of city-wide services. Milwaukee became known everywhere for its philosophy of the lighted schoolhouse, keeping school buildings open after hours for numerous leisure opportunities.

Regardless of age, gender, social class, or ethnic group there were programs for the entire community. The majority of these programs were designed to provide opportunities for participants to socialize and learn new hobbies or pastimes. The indoor centers offered child play areas, adult education, citizenship classes, music lessons, and clubs promoting activities from dance to photography. In some instances they provided individuals the opportunity to excel at areas they were already familiar with. For example, the municipal athletics division carried on a citywide program of competitive sports to supplement the activities conducted at the individual playgrounds and indoor centers.

The success of the Municipal Recreation and Adult Education Department was attributed to two primary factors. First, the dedication and high degree of competence of Enderis and her staff resulted in a very low turnover rate of administration. Secondly, a special tax levy assured continued financial

Dover Street Social Center 1920.
National Recreation Association Archives

support for the school board's program. This financial security ultimately made it possible to maintain a regular staff and for the program's continual expansion.

Under Enderis' leadership, the Milwaukee public recreation department developed an international reputation for its unique programs. Delegates from all over the world came to observe their programs and ask advice. It was said, "Dorothy Enderis became known throughout the world because she demonstrated what a city can do to help its people live happy lives." Rarely did she leave the Milwaukee area, but she did collaborate with the National Recreation Association (NRA) and their apprentice program. Milwaukee is credited for training more apprentices than any other

city at the time. Several of these individuals went on to hold very important positions throughout the recreation movement. In 1932, NRA devoted an entire page in *Recreation* magazine to the excellence of Milwaukee's recreation centers.

Few recreation leaders have received recognition at local, state, and national levels. Dorothy Enderis was the first person to receive a Doctor of Recreation Service, which was awarded to her by Carroll College, Waukesha, WI. In addition, she received an honorary degree of Master of Arts from Laurence College, Appleton, WI, which was given to her "in recognition of her profound sympathy, prophetic vision, administrator skill, and great wisdom." She also was elected an honorary member of

The Lighted School House

"Go to your lighted school house," Milwaukee urges its citizens. "Play-Study-Create."

Milwaukee's lighted school houses make leisure tim show profits in terms of health, knowledge, happiness

ON SEPTEMBER 19th the social centers conducted by the Extension Department, Milwaukee Public Schools, were once more opened to the public with classes, clubs and activities covering a wide variety of subjects.

Classes

Applied arts
Beauty culture
Dressmaking
Furniture making
Home care of sick
Lip reading
Knitting and crocheting
Lamp shade
Miniature aircraft—
  Construction and Flying
Patchwork, quilts

Preparation and serving
  of food
Remodeling of worn gar-
  ments
Leather tooling
Metal work
Needlework
Plaque work
Reed furniture weaving
Rug making
Sewing

Textile painting

Athletic and Game Activities

Gymnasium classes for men and women
Basketball, volley ball, indoor ball for men and women
Boxing, active games, billiards, table games, checker
  clubs, chess clubs
  (Instruction given in beginner's and advanced chess.)

Literary Organizations

Citizenship classes
Debating clubs

English for foreign born
Public speaking

Parliamentary law classes

Music Organizations

Bands, orchestras, mandolin clubs, ukulele clubs, harmonica bands, singing clubs, minstrel troupes, voice
  placement classes.

Dramatic Clubs

Play reading, play production, voice placement, cost
  tume designing, stage setting and scenery
  (Drama clubs will conduct practical work shops
  Their plays will be presented on the Little Theatr
  Nights at the different social centers.)

Dancing Classes

Tap dancing, interpretive dancing, folk dancing, ball
  room dancing

Civic and Social Organizations

Parent-Teacher Associa-
  tions
Civic clubs
Parent training classes
Women's Neighborhood
  clubs

Men's community clubs
Social clubs
Married people's social
  clubs
Girl Scouts
Boy Scouts

Special Community Features

Lectures, recitals, entertainments, motion pictures
Saturday evening dances
Saturday children's entertainments

Reading Rooms and Library Stations

The daily papers are on file in each social center.
  splendid list of the most popular magazines is
  ceived regularly. Five social centers are Milwauke
  Public Library Stations.

Recreation, November 1932

Phi Beta Kappa by the Milwaukee Donner College for the numerous honors bestowed upon her by educational and community organizations.

Among her national services were memberships on the Civilian Advisory Board for the Women's Auxiliary Corps, the Committee for Leisure Time Services of the U.S. Children's Bureau, and the Committee on Social and Religious Activities for Servicemen. Enderis was a popular lecturer at the NRA School and also taught at the University of Wisconsin. After her retirement, the City of Milwaukee honored her by dedicating a recreation area as the Dorothy C. Enderis Playground.

It was on September 30, 1948 that Enderis retired, after serving 36 years in the recreation field—eight years as assistant to the recreation executive, Harold O. Berg, and 28 years as director of the program. She became one of the most highly respected individuals for her diligent fieldwork. She is best known for demonstrating what a city can do to help its citizens lead happy productive lives. What stands out most as one thinks of Enderis and her years of service to the recreation movements, is what she herself said: "I have had an awfully good time at my job."

Adapted from:

Braucher, H. (December, 1948). "Dorothy Enderis Retires," *Recreation*. 393-394.
Butler, G.D. (1965). *Pioneers in public recreation*. Minneapolis, MN: Burgess Publishing Company.
National Recreation Association (November, 1932). The lighted school house, *Recreation*. 388.

Profile photo compliments of Wisconsin Historical Society.

Inducted October 1997

" The professional recreation worker...needs a broad general education, adequate knowledge, skills, and ability in the field of recreation and the proper desire to succeed. "

–Garrett G. Eppley

Garrett G. Eppley
1898-1991

A committed leader and father of the Department of Recreation and Park Administration at Indiana University, Garret G. Eppley was born in Wabash County, IN. Although his national involvement in the park and recreation profession required countrywide travel, he never relinquished his "Hoosier roots." Through the influence of his mother, Eppley enrolled at Manchester College, North Manchester, IN, in 1915. While at Manchester he was appointed director of athletics and an instructor of history. He also served as coach of the college

basketball team and captain of the tennis team. In 1919, Eppley received his Bachelor of Arts degree with a major in history. His graduate studies included a Master's degree in political science from the University of Chicago (1947) and a Doctorate in education with a major in recreation administration from New York University (1953).

Eppley secured his first full-time potion in the fall of 1919, as the principal of the Francesville, Indiana Schools' District. For the next three years he taught courses,

Institute for Parks and Public Lands
INDIANA UNIVERSITY

Named in honor of Dr. Garret G. Eppley, the Eppley Institute was founded in 1993 by Indiana University's Department of Recreation and Park Administration. The mission of the institute is to partner with recreation, park, and public land organizations to enhance access, choice, and quality of natural, cultural, and recreational experiences.
Courtesy of the Eppley Institute

coached athletic teams, and established a wide variety of extra-curricular activities. He also served as president of the Principals' Association and the Athletic Association of Pulaski County. In 1921, the Indiana High School Athletic Association elected him to their Board of Control. Eppley was the youngest member ever to have been elected to this position and was the first to be reelected. From 1922 through 1926 he served on the board and ended his time as president. Eppley took a part-time instructor's position at Whiting, IN, High School from 1922 to 1924 in order to have the opportunity to attend the University of Chicago. At this same time, he worked summers as a playground supervisor. During the summer of 1923, he attended a six-week course at the National Recreation Association's School for Recreation in Chicago. These early experiences nurtured Eppley's professional career in recreation and education.

From 1925 to 1945, Eppley gained practical field and administrative experience through several public agencies and organizations. He served as director of municipal recreation in East Chicago and Evansville, IN; recreation director of the Indiana State Emergency Relief; regional recreation planner for the

National Park Service; and administrator of several United States Organizations (USO) programs. During this time span, Eppley initiated numerous recreation plans consisting of special event activities, construction of recreation facilities, state park naturalist programs; and reptile education demonstrations for Army service members. Under the recommendation of the National Recreation Association's field representative, Lebert Weir, Garrett Eppley began his duties in October 1945 with the development of the recreation and park administration program at Indiana University. He was initially appointed associate professor of recreation education and consultant in recreation for state parks, cities, and schools in Indiana

At Indiana University, Eppley's work was held in high regard. Among his major contributions were the initiation and development of the undergraduate and graduate recreation curriculums. By recruiting a very diverse and highly qualified faculty, Eppley was able to recruit park and recreation students possessing excellent leadership traits, making the department one of the top recreation and park administration departments in the nation. Eppley left his personal imprint on the Indiana University Department

Members of NRPA Administrative Board. From left: First Row–Frank Vaydik, Mrs. Richard M. Colgate, Susan Lee, Mrs. Virginia Wiltbank, Endicott P. Davison, Sal J. Prezioso; Second Row–Courtney Burton, Robert W. Ruhe, J. Austin Smith, James H. Evans, James J. Curtis,Wilburn Stone James; Back Row–James S. Stevens Jr., Stewart G. Case, Conrad L. Wirth, William Penn Mott Jr., William Frederickson, Jr., and Dr. Garrett G. Eppley.
National Recreation and Park Association Archives

of Recreation and Park Administration and its many graduates through his numerous professional writings, his research in municipal recreation finance and administration, his books and articles on public relations techniques, his vision in developing the Great Lakes Park Training Institute, the development and support of the Bradford Woods Outdoor/Education area, and his warmth and personal caring for thousands of students, faculty, and alumni.

Eppley was active in numerous professional organizations serving in leadership positions, including several presidencies in organizations such as the College Recreation Association, the Federation of National Professional Organization for Recreation, American Institute of Park Executives, the American Recreation Society, and the National Recreation Association. He played an important role in helping to formulate and develop the strategy of the American Institute of Park Executives that led to the merger of five National Recreation and Park organizations to form the National Recreation and Park Association. He was a founding member of the Board of Trustees and served on the administrative board (executive committee). This accomplishment took the work of a master strategist and public relations expert, but most of all, the trust of all the leaders in the organizations involved.

Many organizations in the field presented Eppley with their highest awards. Among these are the American Recreation Society Fellowship Award (1958); the American Institute of Park Executives Honorary Fellowship Award (1960); Indiana Park and Recreation Association's "Man of the Year" (1964); the National Recreation and Park Association's Board of Trustees (1965); Manchester College's Honorary Doctor of Laws Degree (1977); and the Society of Park and Recreation Educators' Distinguished Fellow Award (1970). Several awards have been named in his honor.

Eppley was a forceful, dynamic, second generation pioneer in the park and recreation movement. He made a significant and dramatic impact on the park and recreation profession. The influence of his dedication, his philosophical principles, and his personal warmth will continue to live through his students and colleagues. The goal of Eppley's life was to help mankind understand the importance and the value of park and recreation programs in order that man might fulfill and understand their leisure needs.

Adapted from:

American Academy of Park and Recreation Administration. (1983). *Legends of the American Park and Recreation Association*. Downloaded on June 2, 2008 from http://www.aapra.org/legends.html

Craden, M.D. (1975). *Garrett G. Eppley, his life, philosophy, and professional contributions*. Education. dissertation, Indiana University.

" Typical of the man is the fact that all of his civic activities have been performed without thought of personal aggrandizement, but in response to his own conscience and sense of duty to his fellow man. "

–Recreation, February 1951

Inducted October 1991

Robert Garrett
1875 - 1961

Born in Baltimore County, MD, Robert Garrett came from a well-to-do family background. His great grandfather and namesake arrived in Baltimore in the early-1800s and founded the family business of Robert Garrett & Sons, Incorporated. Originally a grocery and consignment company working in the western trade, the family business later evolved into the transportation, banking, and hotel industries, best know for the development of the Baltimore & Ohio Railroad Company.

After the death of his father, Thomas Harrison Garrett in 1888, Garrett, his mother, and two brothers, Horatio W. Garrett and John W. Garrett, spent the next two-and-half years traveling Europe and the Near East. During this time, Garrett developed a life-long curiosity in collecting ancient manuscripts and historic artifacts, consisting of Western and non-Western manuscripts, fragments, and scrolls, originating from Europe, the Near East, Africa, Asia, and Mesoamerica.

Robert Garrett competing in the discus at the 1896 Summer Olympics.
Public Domain, Library of Congress

Robert Garrett's Olympic Medal Records		
1st	1896 Athens	Shot put
1st	1896 Athens	Discus throw
2nd	1896 Athens	High jump
2nd	1896 Athens	Long jump
3rd	1900 Paris	Shot put
3rd	1900 Paris	Standing triple jump

During the early modern Olympics, First and Second place medals were made of silver and Third place contestants did not receive a medal.

Garrett's deep interest in recreation stems back to his own natural ability as an athlete. Garrett excelled in track and field events as an undergraduate at Princeton. He was captain of the team in both his junior and senior years. In 1896 he organized and financed a trip for himself and three classmates to the first modern Olympic

Cover of the official report of 1896 Athens Summer Olympics, officially know as Games of the I Olympiad.
Public Domain, Library of Congress

Games in Athens, Greece. Garrett stood out among the competitors, winning two first place and two second place medals. One of his first place medals was in the discus throw, an event in which he had never before competed. He also competed in the 1900 Olympic Games in Paris, France, in the shot put, standing triple jump, and tug of war events.

Upon receiving his Bachelor of Arts degree from Princeton in 1897, Garrett joined the family banking firm of Robert Garrett & Sons and became one of Baltimore's most prominent businessmen. Throughout his life, he maintained contact with his alma mater, serving as class president for 64 years and on the Board of Trustees.

Princeton track and field team, Garrett pictured in center with shot put.
Public Domain, Library of Congress

In 1905 he was elected a Life Trustee of Princeton University. Garrett donated to Princeton University his collection of more than 10,000 manuscripts, including 16 rare and beautiful examples of Byzantine art in 1942.

Garrett played an intricate part in the development and financing of Baltimore's public recreation. In 1903 he established the first of several open-air gymnasiums in the city and organized sporting events among youth in the public parks. He was a founding member of the Public Athletic League in 1907, which he served as president. The following year he invited Lee Hanmer, co-organizer of the Boy Scouts of America, to Baltimore to help establish an expanded program of playgrounds, public gymnasiums, and athletic games for youth. In 1922 the Public Athletic League and the Children's Playground Association joined forces to development the Playground Athletic League, which later became the Baltimore Department of Recreation and Parks. Garrett's service as chairman to these organizations was successive throughout their development until 1948.

Only an individual with a dedicated sense of civic responsibility would have served his city so continuously, and his long tenure bore testimony to Garrett's high standards and exceptional ability. His record in Baltimore was matched by his demonstrated loyalty to the National Recreation Association, for he was first elected a member of its Board of Directors in 1910, became third vice-president in 1916, and served as its chairman from 1941 until his retirement in 1950. In a letter to Garrett, Joseph Prendergast, executive director of athlete himself, he maintained throughout his life. Garrett was one of the first of his generation to realize that public recreation was not a luxury but a necessity. In a life of effort to meet this need he was a pioneer, a foundation builder, and, in a sense the embodiment of the public's conscience. Garrett holds the distinction of being the first lay worker to receive the R. Tait Mackenzie Award from the American Alliance for Health, Physical Education, Recreation and Dance "for outstanding work in health, physical education, and recreation."

Adapted from:

Butler, G.D. (1965). *Pioneers in public recreation*. Minneapolis, MN: Burgess Publishing Company.

Hartsoe, C. (2007). *Building better communities: The story of the National Recreation Association (1906-1965)*. Champaign, IL: Sagamore Publishing.

National Recreation Association (February, 1951). Robert Garrett retires, *Recreation*. 470.

Garrett was responsible for bringing the Boy Scouts of America and the Young Men's Christian Association to the Baltimore area.
Enoch Pratt Free Library, City of Baltimore

the Association, wrote: "The Board of the National Recreation Association is justly proud of your 40 years of splendid, unselfish service as one of its members and of the nine years within that period during which you served as chairman of the Board. Times without number, your broad experience and personal knowledge in the fields of recreation, sports, education, finance, and the cultural arts have strengthened the deliberation of the Board and given its members a sense of renewed confidence."

Garrett will best be remembered for his work in behalf of public recreation. He not only contributed his time to assure success, but often donated his personal finances. Recreation was an interest which, as an

Inducted October 1991

"Our jobs were healthful, natural, and in the public service, and we served a great and select social purpose in our custodianship and management of these 'national jewels.'"

—Lemuel A. Garrison

Lemuel A. Garrison
1903 - 1984

Lemuel Alonzo "Lon" Garrison truly had a love for the national parks and high ideals for public service. Garrison was a personification of the blazing idealism of Stephen Mather and Horace Albright, authors of the 1916 *National Park Service Organic Act* and first directors of the National Park Service (NPS). Through his years of service as a park ranger, administrator, educator, and professional in park organizations, Garrison made the Mather-Albright idealism a reality. Today, billions of people throughout the world are able to enjoy well managed parks based on the knowledge, skills, and education Garrison imparted with all who shared in his life.

In 1926 Garrison graduated from Stanford University, CA, with a Bachelor of Science degree in applied psychology and economics. Three years later, he began his 40 year career with the NPS. His first job was a forest service fire ranger at the Chugach National Forest in Alaska. Located in the mountains surrounding Prince William Sound, Garrison's duties included protecting and managing 5.4 million acres

Garrison, superintendent of Yellowstone National Park, 1957.
National Park Service Historic Photograph Collection

of his Stanford psychology professors, he developed a questionnaire to gather hard data on counting the numbers of visitors and establishing a list of their activities while visiting Yosemite. This technique and practice became commonplace in most levels of recreation planning. The Yosemite research information was used as part of the Mission 66 Program the National Park Service initiated in 1954.

Mission 66 set a goal of refurbishing and adding new park facilities, establishing manpower standards, sanitation, roads, concession roles, employee housing, and recruiting and training personnel. Director Conrad Wirth successfully convinced the Congress and President Eisenhower

of timber in the second largest forest of the NPS. His colleagues, employees, and park visitors credited him with developing an awareness of economic and social responsibilities for wise land use.

In 1932 Garrison became a seasonal ranger for Lodgepole Campground in Sequoia National Park. Established in 1890, Sequoia National Park is California's first national park and America's second oldest. Sequoia presented an alternate use of the forest as a means for public recreation. The appropriateness of park preservation became a value Garrison shared throughout his career and he became an advocate for establishing recreation space in the National Parks.

Garrison pioneered the development of resource protective skills through people management. During 1935 he became a permanent ranger in Yosemite National Park. He managed a campground in 1938 and began to deal with crowding and resource deterioration. With the help

The Making of a Ranger chronicled Garrison's experiences with the National Park Service.

that the National Park Service needed this program. Garrison was appointed to chair the Mission's steering committee. The management techniques resulting from Garrison's research were used in the Mission 66 Program to limit the use to other less critical alternative sites, and providing a diversity of recreation opportunities.

Between 1939 and 1964 Garrison was assistant superintendent at Glacier and Grand Canyon National Parks, super-intendent at Hopewell Village National Historic Site, Big Bend, and Yellowstone National Parks. During that time he served as Chief Ranger in Washington DC and received a Meritorious Service Award from the Department of the Interior. Garrison became a Regional Director in the Midwestern Region, Omaha, NE, in 1963 and transferred to the Northeastern Region in 1965 to serve in the same capacity. He received the National Pugsley Medal in 1968 for his efforts in conservation and in 1970, became Director of the Albright Training Academy at Grand Canyon National Park. In 1973 Garrison retired and became president of the National Conference on State Parks where he conceived the idea of "partnerships" between state parks and the NPS.

Garrison's leadership included membership in the National Recreation and Park Association, its council, and the Board of Trustees. He was a recipient of the Award of Excellence from the National Conference on State Parks in

Three horseman start out a seven-day trip to the Two Ocean Plateau and Heart Lake Basin of Yellowstone National Park: Associate Director Eivind Scoyen, Director Conrad L. Wirth, and Superintendent Lemuel A. "Lon" Garrison.
National Geographic Society

1972, Distinguished Service Award from the National Society for Park Resources in 1976, and was active in the Society for Park and Recreation Educators. He completed his career as a visiting professor at the Department of Recreation and Park Administration, Texas A&M University.

Garrison's legacy to the park and recreation profession is summarized in his book, *The Making of a Ranger*. "We have an obligation to be faithful to our park preservation trusts and to the Congress and the citizens who worked to establish it. At the same time, we must be honest with users and politicians about our judgments and decisions. We cannot always win, but we can keep our own integrity and honor." He believed that the American people cannot wander too far from the great outdoors without losing character, strength, and orientation. His conviction was more than an impulse to preserve trees, or natural phenomena, or wilderness, or to contemplate man's relationship with the earth. Garrison was dedicated to the understanding combined with the preservation of an environment, which he was convinced was essential to American's spiritual well-being, and to the nation.

Adapted from:

Crompton, J.L. (2008). *Twentieth century champions of parks and conservation: The Pugsley award recipients 1928-1964. Volume I.* Champaign, IL: Sagamore Publishing.

Garrison, L.A. (1983). *The making of a ranger: Forty years with the National Parks.* Salt Lake City, UT: Howe Brothers.

Heath, E.H. (1991). *In memory of Lon Garrison.* Unpublished eulogy.

National Recreation and Park Association. *Recreation and Park Hall of fame nomination form.* Unpublished document.

" The individual is more completely revealed in play than in any other way and conversely, play has a greater shaping power over the character and nature of man than any activity. "

–Luther H. Gulick

Inducted October 1988

Luther H. Gulick
1865-1918

The son of a physician, Luther Halsey Gulick was born in Honolulu, HI. Due to his father's missionary occupation, he traveled overseas to such countries as Spain, Italy, and Japan. Upon returning to the United States in 1880, Gulick studied at Oberlin Academy, Sargent School of Physical Training, and New York University, where he earned his Doctor of Medicine in 1889.

In the course of pursuing a medical degree, Gulick began his physical education career with the Jackson, MI, YMCA. During the summer of 1887 he headed the first summer school of "Special Training for Gymnasium Instructors" at the Young Men's Christian Education's Training School, now Springfield College, where he taught for 13 years. Interested in the traits and qualities essential in physical activity and gaming, he challenged one of his students, James Naismith, to develop an indoor winter sport. The game became known as basketball and Gulick was inducted in 1959 to the Naismith Memorial Basketball Hall of Fame for his contributions to its early development. In addition to his academic position, he was secretary of the American Association for the Advancement of Physical Education from 1892 to 1893.

YMCA Training School, taken between 1904 and 1910.
Springfield College, Babson Library, Archives and Special Collections

At the turn of the twentieth century, Luther Gulick was among the leading forces for several physical education associations. He was the president of the American Physical Education Association between 1903 and 1906, president of the Public School Training Society between 1905 and 1908, helped organize the American School Hygiene Association in 1907, and originated the concept for a national organization to provide leadership in the growing interest of play. The Playground Association of America was established in April 1906 and Luther Gulick was elected their first president. He served in this position from 1906 to 1908.

Under Gulick's leadership, the Playground Association of America made amazing progress. According to Howard Braucher, "His personal qualities were such, his ability as a speaker, his vividness

Luther Gulick (center) is posing with students in 1890.
Springfield College, Babson Library, Archives and Special Collections

of description at private interviews, his unfailing enthusiasm, all were such that the new movement made a very great appeal to the country. He emphasized the value of publicity and of having the names and pictures of important people associated with the new movement."

In the introduction to his book, *A Philosophy of Play* (1920), Gulick set forth three conclusions he had reached based on his study of play:

I. The individual is more completely revealed in play than in any other way; and conversely, play has a greater shaping power over the character and nature of man than has any one other activity.
II. A people most truly reveal themselves in the character of its pleasures.
III. The individual is more an agent in life than a directing force.

In 1914 Gulick and his wife, Charlotte Vetter Gulick, founded the Camp Fire Girls. They used their summer camps, Camp Timanous and Camp Wohelo, as models to test and develop programs and activities. Their goal was to promote physical fitness and education through recreational activities. Luther Gulick was named the Campfire Girls' first president

Luther Gulick designed the YMCA logo, a triangle expressing the relationship of spirit, mind, and body.

and served as its head and guiding spirit until his death in 1918.

Gulick had a significant impact in the early stages of the physical education and recreation movement. Known as one of the great innovators, Gulick was able to introduce new ideas with what was widely accepted, progressing both fields. Since 1923 the American Alliance for Health, Physical Education, Recreation and Dance (AAPHERD) has annually awarded the Luther Halsey Gulick Medal as its highest honor to a distinguished leader in the Alliance's fields.

Adapted from:

Butler, G.D. (1965). *Pioneers in public recreation*. Minneapolis, MN: Burgess Publishing Company.
Gulick, L.H. (1920). *A philosophy of play*. New York: Charles Scribner's Sons.
Ibrahim, H. (1989). *Pioneers in leisure and recreation*. Reston, VA: American Alliance for Health, Physical Education, Recreation, and Dance.

President Theodore Roosevelt hosted the Playground Association of America at the White House in 1906 and served as an honorary president.

"All people need some recreation, and all patients are people. Hence, all patients need recreation to some degree."

–Beatrice H. Hill

Inducted October 1999

Beatrice H. Hill
1914-1993

While visiting a relative receiving treatment for tuberculosis in 1940, Beatrice Hill observed the lack of recreation activities and services available to hospitalized patients. Recognizing this void in their treatment, the effects of excessive boredom, and the lack of stimulation, she volunteered to serve as consultant for recreation rehabilitation services in the Institute of Hospital Medicine of the Goldwater Memorial Hospital in New York City. Shortly thereafter, she met Dr. Howard Rusk, director of the Institute of Physical Medicine and Rehabilitation

and together they worked to establish recreation programs throughout all of New York City's municipal hospitals.

In 1953 Hill was employed by the National Recreation Association(NRA) to direct its consulting service for the emerging field of hospital recreation. This service was later renamed the NRA Consulting Service on Recreation for the Ill and Handicapped. Over the years, the NRA's interest in this area was only marginal. However, one of the first committees created by the Playground Association

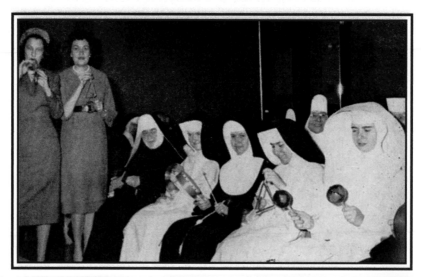

Catholic Charities of New York City staged a six-session workshop for nun-administrators of nursing homes and homes for the aged in Connecticut, Pennsylvania, New Jersey, and New York. A session on recreation was conducted by the NRA Consulting Service on Recreation for the Ill and Handicapped. *Recreation*, March 1959

of America in 1907 focused on play in institutions. Despite this early interest, it was not until 1953, with the employment of Hill, that the NRA assumed a major role in promoting recreation services for the ill and handicapped. This new service provided advice and consultation to individuals and organizations including hospitals, nursing homes, special agencies, and community groups on services for the handicapped. In addition to organizing training workshops and carrying out survey research, the consulting service answered over 200 inquiries each month.

In the eight years Hill served on the NRA staff, there was a phenomenal increase in the recognition and acceptance of the concept of recreation as a major force in the rehabilitation of the ill and handicapped. Likewise, there was a corresponding increase in the demands on the NRA for consulting services on recreation for the ill and handicapped.

Hill produced the first educational film on the therapeutic value of recreation for

patients in non-government hospitals. The film, entitled "So Much for So Little," was financed by a grant from the Hofheimer Foundation. It shows, in dramatic form, how a volunteer worker discovers that recreation in a general civilian hospital contributes to a better patient morale. One of the highlights of the film is an appeal made by Howard A. Rusk, M.D., director of the Institute of Physical Medicine and Rehabilitation and Associate Editor of *The New York Times*, for more community and professional interest in this new field.

Beatrice Hill was also the author of one of the first publications on hospital recreation. *Starting a Recreation Program in a Civilian Hospital* was designed to help the neophyte in a civilian hospital to understand and plan effectively for hospital recreation.

She edited a monthly column in *Recreation* magazine entitled "Hospital Recreation" and later renamed "Rx for the Ill and Handicapped." This column carried news on interesting developments

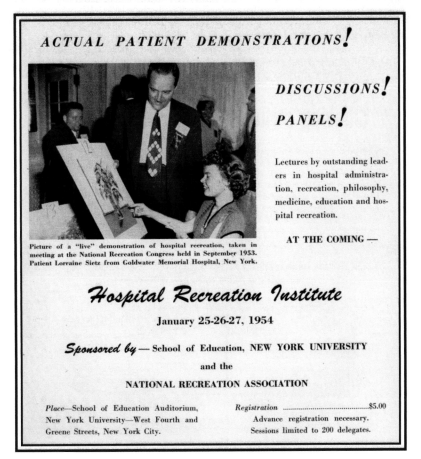

A flyer for one of Hill's programs to promote recreation in hospitals and care facilities. *Recreation*, January 1954

in programs, research, and personnel concerned with recreation for the ill and handicapped.

Hill was awarded an honorary master's degree from Springfield College in 1958 in recognition of her pioneering and outstanding work in creating recreation opportunities for the ill and handicapped.

With support from the Avalon Foundation and a grant from the Office of Vocational Rehabilitation, Hill established Comeback, Inc., a non-profit organization dedicated to "promote through recreation the social rehabilitation of the aged, ill, and handicapped." Its impact was significant by providing the first scholarship program for

university training in therapeutic recreation and influencing the development of standards for personnel and registration of therapeutic recreation specialists. Largely as a result of her success and the realization on the part of the federal government that it should include recreation services as part of its matrix of human service programs, the Office of Vocational Rehabilitation in 1963 began awarding scholarships and financial support for faculty positions in a select number of universities offering graduate work in therapeutic recreation. Four years later, Comeback, Inc., was dissolved, its work complete.

Beatrice Hill's life was one of dedication. Like so many pioneers, she was not professionally trained in the field she influenced, but because of her energy and vision the field prospered. She demonstrated the value of a consulting service, promoted the need for professional standards, and influenced the federal government to accept therapeutic recreation as an allied health profession. As important as these actions were, perhaps her most significant accomplishment was the promotion and recognition of the concept that the community is the natural setting for recreation programs to serve those with disabilities, that it can help in reintegration, and that recreation programs should be accessible to all citizens. Because of this advocacy, millions are the beneficiaries of her vision and effort.

Adapted from:

Avedon, Elliott M. (1974) *Therapeutic recreation service.* Englewood Cliffs, NJ: Prentice Hall, Inc.
Hill, B. (1953-1961). "Hospital Capsules," *Recreation.* National Recreation Association.

Inducted October 1991

"There is no reason why every center should not hum with activity every day and every night—no reason short of your capacity to bring about such a result."

–George Hjelte

George Hjelte
1893-1979

Few executives have done more to promote efficient administration of municipal recreation than George Hjelte. The son of Swedish immigrants, Hjelte grew up in the San Francisco Bay area. Majoring in economics and physical education, he attended the University of California, Berkeley. While in college he was an outstanding athlete, gaining selection as All Pacific Coast Conference and All American in 1917 for basketball. Upon graduation, he entered officer training at the Presidio in San Francisco and later was commissioned a second lieutenant. He served with the allied forces in Europe during World War I and earned the Belgium War Cross for bravery. He was discharged in England with the rank of major where he stayed abroad for a short period and studied at Cambridge University. Returning to California in 1919, he continued his graduate work at Berkeley. During these graduate years, he served as a graduate teaching assistant in physical education.

The
Administration of
Public Recreation

By GEORGE HJELTE

Superintendent of Recreation, City of Los Angeles;
Formerly Superintendent of Recreation,
Westchester County, New York

NEW YORK
THE MACMILLAN COMPANY

Prior to the war, Hjelte held a part-time position as a high school athletic coach and served full-time as a director of boys' work. Upon his graduation in 1919 he was named assistant state supervisor of physical education in the California school system. Two years later he was also appointed superintendent of recreation in Berkeley. Recreation became his primary interest; however, after five years at Berkeley in the combined position, Hjelte was appointed superintendent of recreation in Los Angeles in 1926. He worked continuously in this city, except for a three-year term in a similar position in Westchester County, NY, while serving as recreation officer for the Joint Army and Navy Committee on Welfare and Recreation during World War II in 1942. The tremendous expansion of Los Angeles' recreation facilities, and programs are a testimonial to his leadership and administrative ability.

The people of Los Angeles demonstrated their appreciation of Hjelte's committed work in recreation by their repeated support of tax referenda. During the depression, in 1937, the recreation tax was increased two cents for each $100 of assessment. It was the only one of 30 proposed amendments to receive a unanimous vote from the city council. This financial support was largely due to the active backing of organizations such as the Parent-Teacher Associations and the Woman's Clubs.

Prior to most executives, Hjelte understood the importance of keeping accurate reports as a means of checking the effectiveness of departmental operations. He urged his staff to keep precise program records. This information was used to evaluate such factors as program participation, safety, and distances people travel to reach the recreation centers. Hjelte realized these statistics helped gain program support by proving that a dollar's worth of service was being rendered for each dollar invested. The preparation and administration of budgets and methods of financial record keeping were subjects of special interest to him, and he shared his ideas through the preparation of material distributed by the National Recreation Association. His book, *The Administration of Public Recreation*, published in 1940, was one of the first texts to focus on the subject and proved a valuable guide to recreation authorities in establishing sound administrative procedures. A completely revised edition, entitled *Public Administration of Park and Recreation Services*, appeared in 1963.

Among the unusual facility developments made possible through a 1947 bond issue were a prize-winning mountain camp for girls, a workshop for the development of experimental equipment, a drama center, and Travel Town, an area in which many

Presidents Conference on fitness of American Youth. Held in Annapolis. From left: Joseph Prendergast, NRA; Ted Banks, The Athletic Institute; Mr. Nixon; George Hjelte, Los Angeles Department of Recreation and Parks; George Sargisson, Recreation Promotion & Services, Wilmington, DE.
Recreation, September 1956

famous railroad locomotives were given a home. Hjelte's standing and authority were further enhanced when in 1947 the park and recreation sections were consolidated into the Recreation and Parks Department. Hjelte was named its general manager. Again, in 1957 a $39,500,000 bond was issued for the acquisition, construction, and improvement of the city's park and recreation system. This bond made it possible for the expansion of playgrounds, regional and community parks, a new zoo, swimming pools, golf courses, and maintenance facilities.

Few if any recreation executives have rendered more generous service to the movement through participation in committee projects. When he retired in 1962 he had served on governmental committees under every President from Herbert Hoover to John F. Kennedy. His cooperation with the National Recreation Association was demonstrated repeatedly by his willingness to accept committee assignments. When the Association established the National Advisory Council composed of the chairmen of its district and special advisory committees, Hjelte was chosen to head it. While in Westchester County he served as an instructor of

recreation administration at the National Recreation School. As an active charter member of the American Recreation Society, he was elected its second president.

Hjelte received many honors in recognition of his distinguished public service. Perhaps none were more significant than that bestowed upon him by the National Recreation Association, which in 1962 elected him a member of their Board of Directors. When he retired in 1962, the City of Los Angeles appointed Hjelte as a consultant in the development of their modern zoo. Through his early use of statistics, budgets, and program evaluations, Hjelte is credited as one of the early leaders in the development of planning standards for the park and recreation field. His executive insight beyond doubt advanced the aptitude of the profession.

Adapted from:

Butler, G.D. (1965). *Pioneers in public recreation.* Minneapolis, MN: Burgess Publishing Company.
Ibrahim, H. (1989). *Pioneers in leisure and recreation.* Reston, VA: American Alliance for Health, Physical Education, Recreation, and Dance.

Inducted October 2005

"Make up your minds that you know what you are doing. Like people and learn how to work with people. "

−Kathryn E. Krieg

Kathryn E. Krieg
1904-1999

Originally from Indiana, Kathryn Krieg grew up in Omaha, NE. Upon graduating high school, one of her teachers persuaded her to continue her education and in 1926 she earned a Bachelor of Arts degree, majoring in physical education, from the University of Nebraska. In 1927 she attended the National Recreation Association's Recreation Leadership School. During a video interview, the American Academy of Park and Recreation Administration's Living Legends Series, Krieg reflected on this experience, "This was a chance to see

New York City. I lived in the Bronx in a settlement house and worked there too and did office work for a half day for the National Recreation Association." Krieg was among the first class of students to graduate from this one-year training school.

In 1928 Krieg returned to Iowa and became the director for Girls Recreation in Council Bluffs. Due to a lack of program funding, nine months later she was headed for the Chicago-Milwaukee area for a full-time position when Lewis Barrett, Des Moines Playground director, asked her

Krieg in the car she used to "check on the playgrounds."
Photo compliments of the Irwin Family

to stay and work for the summer. This temporary position became a 46-year career in Des Moines for Krieg. After the departure of Barrett in 1931, Krieg became the superintendent of recreation and eventually retired as the director of recreation in 1974.

Before the term, "collaborate" was a buzz word, Krieg created alliances with partners from all lines of public and private agencies and organizations such as the parks, schools, adult education, conservation groups, YMCA, YWCA, Campfire Boys and Girls, Boy and Girl Scouts, Parent Teacher Association, Federation of Women's Clubs, and settlement houses to name a few. Here are a few examples of her outstanding and lasting contributions:

• Development of one of the first organized playgrounds in the country through efforts of the Chancey DePew Club

• Introduced square dancing for adults needing a positive diversion during the Great Depression.

• Operated the largest adult softball program in the state and was later inducted into the Des Moines Softball Hall of Fame

• Maintained a positive partnership with the schools, beginning in the 30s by sharing facilities and running year-round community centers in the public schools

• Organized training through the annual Governor's Conference on Recreation for literally thousands of volunteer leaders

• Created a Des Moines tradition, Beggars Night, in response to the growing number of vandalism reports on Halloween. Beggars Night became the night for tricks or treats for kids' safety and separated it from adult Halloween parties

• Operated Camp Dodge Swimming Pool on the Iowa National Guard property

Kathryn Krieg's greatest accolades came from people who approached her to reminisce about participating in recreation activities.
The Des Moines Register, October 26, 2000

so that the public had use of this pool, the second largest in the world, when the war ended

- Operated Ewing Park Day Camp, a full-day camp for kids to learn camping and outdoor recreation skills, which became a "right of passage" for kids growing up in Des Moines.

Krieg's dedication to the recreation field was exemplified by her diligent commitment to create and develop strong professional organizations. She was a Charter Member of the original Iowa Association of Municipal Recreation Executives, serving as its second president in 1947. This organization later became the Iowa Park and Recreation Society and finally the Iowa Park and Recreation Association. In 1966 Krieg was presented with an Award of Merit and voted a life time member of the Iowa Park and Recreation Association, in recognition of her efforts.

In addition, Krieg was a pioneer at the national level where she helped to organized the Society of Recreation Workers of America, Inc., which later became the American Recreation Society and finally the American Park and Recreation Society. She worked as the Midwest Geographical Representative of the American Recreation Society in concert with field staff. In 1965 the American Park and Recreation Society recognized Krieg with its highest honor when it selected her to receive their "Fellow Award." During this same year, she was also among the founding members of the Board of Trustees for the National Recreation and Park Association. She felt a personal victory in seeing that "Recreation" came first in the Association's name.

On March 20, 1974, Krieg was presented a plaque by the Iowa Park and Recreation Association which read; "Distinguished Service Award to Kathryn E. Krieg for Outstanding Professionalism in 46 Years of Dedicated and Unselfish Community Service." She was modest and humble about her significant accomplishments, which not only shaped professional organizations, but

July 1992, Great Lakes Regional Council Awards Dinner: Kathryn Krieg is honored and receives a replica of the NRPA Charter. Also pictured are Dave Sacco, Ohio, Christine Page, Iowa, and Walt Johnson, Great Lakes Regional Council Chair.
Courtesy of Christine Page, Fundbrokers, LLC.

also her contributions to the quality of life in her community.

Of all her accomplishments, Krieg told the *Journal of Iowa Parks and Recreation*, that she derived the most enjoyment from seeing others have fun. "You shouldn't just try to be an administrator...you've got to be interested in people." It is often said success in life is not measured by financial wealth or position, but rather by the number of people you have touched. As one of the few women who held a major administrative position in recreation during the early years, this statement exemplifies Krieg who was focused on the total holistic needs and wellbeing of the people in her community, state, and nation.

Adapted from:

American Academy of Park and Recreation Administration. (1994). *Legends of the American Park and Recreation Association.* Downloaded on March 23, 2008 from http://www.aapra.org/legends.html

Kremenak, C. (1974). Thanks to Kathryn. *Journal of Iowa Parks and Recreation*, 3(2), 1.

National Recreation and Park Association (May 2005). *Nomination for Kathryn E. Krieg for the Recreation and Park Hall of Fame.* Unpublished document.

National Recreation and Park Association (July, 1999). Obituaries, *Parks & Recreation*.

*We do not cease playing because
we are old; we grow old because
we cease playing.*

–Joseph Lee

Inducted October 1988

Joseph Lee
1862-1937

Known as the "Father of the Playground Movement," Joseph Lee is among the most recognized pioneers in the recreation movement. Growing up in Boston, MA, in the mid-nineteenth century he often filled evenings playing games such as Robbers and Policemen, Prisoner's Base, and Hi-Spy with childhood friends know as the "Crowd." Perhaps these activities contributed more than any to the development of Lee's beliefs in the importance of play and recreation.

During the period of 1883 through 1887, Lee completed his undergraduate studies at Harvard and pursued a degree from Harvard Law School. In 1891 he was admitted to the bar. Lee soon became committed to a life of public service and never practiced law. He instead used his legal knowledge base in 1897 when he founded the Massachusetts Civic League in order to legislate laws that progressed community and social equality.

Joseph Lee in 1883.
Recreation, December 1937

Lee's first activity dealing with play-grounds was an 1882 survey conducted by the Family Welfare Society of Boston. He studied play opportunities in several congested neighborhoods and in the South End. When he witnessed boys arrested for playing in the streets he was shocked and commented, "It was as if the boys had been arrested for living." In 1898, Lee helped create the first "model" playground. Located at Columbus Avenue in a desolate neighborhood, the several-acre playground included a corner for small children, a boys' section, a field for sports, 260 individual gardens, and two old stables remodeled for indoor activities. The Columbus Avenue Playground was said to be the very first of the large playgrounds. Its success was widely acclaimed and led to a calling for a playground meeting in 1906 at Washington, D.C., by the Playground Association of America (PAA). It was said Lee changed the whole course of the play movement when he sent the PAA a check for $25,000 to support their plight.

PAA was dedicated to improving the human environment through park, recreation, and leisure opportunities. PAA was renamed the Playground and Recreation Association of America (PRAA) in 1911 and later became the National Recreation Association (NRA) in 1930. Joseph Lee was a major influence in these early predecessors of the National Park and Recreation Association. He served as vice-president and president of PRAA, and president of NRA.

Joseph Lee was instrumental in having the NRA establish the National Recreation School, which offered a one-year course for carefully selected college graduates. He served as president and a lecturer at the school, many of whose graduates won top executive positions in the recreation field. The first World War brought to the Association the tremendous task of forming and operating the War Camp

Major General Clarence R. Richards decorates Joseph Lee with the Distinguished Service Medal.
Recreation, December 1937

Recreation Movement Celebrates Birthday

Reading from left to right: Otto T. Mallery, President of Philadelphia Playground Association; Mrs. Charles D. Lanier, Greenwich, Conn.; F. S. Titsworth, Attorney, New York City; Gustavus T. Kirby, President of Public Schools Athletic League, New York City; Joseph Lee, Boston, President of the Association; President Hoover; H. S. Braucher, Secretary of the Association; Carl E. Milliken, Former Governor of Maine; Mrs. Arthur E. Cummer, Jacksonville, Florida; Austin E. Griffiths, Former Justice of the Superior Court, Seattle, Washington; Mrs. Edward W. Biddle, Carlisle, Pa.; J. C. Walsh, Publisher, New York City; Wm. C. Butterworth, President Chamber of Commerce of the United States.

Twenty-Fifth Anniversary Meeting
Board of Directors National Recreation Association

The White House, Washington, D. C.
April 13, 1931

I AM glad to welcome the directors of the National Recreation Association at the White House on this occasion. The Association was organized at the White House twenty-five years ago, and it is a most fitting place for your twenty-fifth anniversary meeting.

"I have followed the work of the Association for many years. It has taken a most significant and a magnificent part in the whole recreational development of the country. Its work today is of increasing importance because of the growing congestion of cities, on one hand, and the increasing leisure of our people, on the other. The whole recreational movement is one not only vital to public health, but it is vital to public welfare. The growing congestion of the cities presents constantly new problems of physical and moral and mental training of children, on one hand, and the growing leisure by shortened hours of labor presents increasing problems in provision of opportunity for proper use of increasing leisure for adults. Many less problems in government arise which concern people while they are at work than

while they are at leisure. They do not often go to jail for activities when they are on their jobs. Most of our problems arise when the people are off of the job. Every progress in constructive recreation for leisure time not only improves health, but also morals.

"The Federal government, during the period of the Association's activities and to a considerable degree due to the efforts of the Association, has developed in itself a great number of recreational activities. I assume that the growth of social aspects of government will increase the interest of the government in recreational questions, and we need the assistance of the Association in directing these policies. If there is anything that we can do to cooperate with the Association in any direction you will find a most hearty welcome to the views of the Association in every section of the government.

"I wish to express to you the most profound admiration that I hold for the work of the Association and to extend to you my best wishes for its further development."—Herbert Hoover,
President of the United States

58

Community Service (WCCS) to provide off-duty recreation opportunities for service personnel. Lee was named to the Commissions of Training Camp Activities of the War and Navy Departments, became president of WCCS, and worked tirelessly to further the war efforts.

Lee was also one of the recreation movement's most prolific writers. A mere listing of the titles of some of his early publications illustrates their range and suggests their influence upon the movement; *Play as the School of the Citizen, Why Have Playgrounds? Sunday Play, Play as an Antidote to Civilization, Play for Home, Playgrounds in the United States, Play as a Landscape*, and *Playground Education. Play in Education,* Mr. Lee's most ambitious and best-known work, appeared in 1915. Educators and recreation leaders immediately hailed the book as a masterpiece.

Adapted from:

Butler, G.D. (1965). *Pioneers in public recreation.* Minneapolis, MN: Burgess Publishing Company.
National Recreation Association (December, 1937). Special issue dedicated to Joseph Lee. *Recreation.* New York.

THE WHITE HOUSE
WASHINGTON

May 26, 1938

Dear Dr. Finley:

I am heartily in accord with the idea of setting aside a special time to pay tribute to the life and work of Joseph Lee. His simplicity, his humor, his philosophy, his integrity, his courage endeared him to all who came to know him and work with him and these were legion.

He saw that for children, play was the serious business of life; that for youth recreation was an important school for citizenship; and that for adults leisure rightly used meant the difference between mere existence and fruitful living. The genius of Joseph Lee lay not alone in seeing these things. He used what he was and what he had to forge the machinery necessary to make them real in American life.

Today in the far flung communities of a great nation children are happier, youth is better served, and man and women have a chance to live more richly because of the life and work of Joseph Lee. No greater tribute could be paid than to have a share in helping to strengthen and build further this vital part of our community and of our national life.

Very sincerely
yours,
(Signed)
Franklin D. Roosevelt

Dr. John H. Finley
President,
National Recreation Association,
315 Fourth Avenue,
New York, NY

National Park and Recreation Association Archives

Inducted October 1991

"The ultimate strength of the National Recreation Association lies in the devotion and civic spirit of thousands of lay men and women on boards, committees, and foundations who steadily hold the line and keep advancing it."

–Otto T. Mallery

Otto Tod Mallery
1880-1956

Born in Willets Point, NY, in 1881, Otto Tod Mallery graduated with a Bachelor of Arts degree from Princeton University in 1902 and pursued graduate studies at the University of Pennsylvania and Columbia University. Known as an economist and gentleman, he devoted himself to the advancement of recreation in Philadelphia, throughout the United States, and the world. Mallery experienced great joy and value from participating in recreation and strived to extend opportunities for others to enjoy similar experiences. Among his favorite pastimes were painting, dancing, and playing the bass violin in his family's chamber music ensemble.

Mallery, a citizen volunteer, was a guiding founder and charter member of the Philadelphia Playground Association, formed in 1907. Philadelphia is distinguished for having one of the nation's oldest private recreation agencies. Mallery chaired many of the Association's committees and served as treasurer from 1910 to 1925, when he was elected president. One of Mallery's early attempts to promote public recreation in Philadelphia was in 1909 when he persuaded the mayor to appoint a Public Playgrounds Commission. Their focus was to examine the local recreation facilities and recommend the best utilization to service the community. Within the Commission, an official Playgrounds Committee was authorized to develop and manage the local municipal playgrounds and recreation centers. The Committee was soon superseded by a Board of Recreation with broader functions, where Mallery was named one of the original board members and served as secretary from 1912 to 1915.

In 1918 after the supervisor of recreation resigned, Philadelphia's Mayor, Thomas B. Smith, wished to reward Eduard R. Gudehus with the position for helping him politically. He ordered the Civil Service Commission to reissue the announcement for the supervisor's examination and to eliminate the experience qualifications originally established by the board of Recreation. Mayor Smith threatened board members with expulsion if they objected. Several refused and they were immediately dismissed from their positions. Upon reappointment of the board, Gudehus was elected the new supervisor of recreation. Mallery made a thorough report of the incident and a detailed deposition calling for the arrest of the mayor for committing the crime of misbehavior and misdemeanor in office. Mallery's efforts were widely praised as a courageous civic action, however failed to have mayor Smith arrested or removed from office and the new board remained intact.

1927 began a period of originating new services and expansion of the Playgrounds Association. Succeeding years marked the broadening of programs and services, including art appreciation programs, costumed storytellers, the first "totlot" playgrounds, indoor playhouses, safe-coasting hills, use of city squares as playgrounds, learn-to-swim campaigns, city-wide music festivals, and institutes to train recreation leaders. This type of expansion continued through Mallery's long service, and each year further plans enabled an increasing number of local citizens to participate in a wider range of creative and cultural activities. Advances in the 1940's, aside from war emergency programs, included the playlot movement inaugurated in cooperation with Federal and Municipal Government Agencies, development of youth councils, recreation for older adults, and a conference of local recreation agencies on "Recreation, a Community Responsibility."

The name of the Association was changed in 1946 to the Philadelphia Recreation Association. The original charter was amended and functions changed from that of an operational agency to that of a recreational/promotional agency "to further the expansion and improvement of public recreation" and "to manage, direct, and/or operate any recreation projects for the benefit of the public." Two years later, Mallery retired as the Association's president. Upon his departure, the Association distinguished his 40 years of leadership and service by honoring him with Chairman Emeritus status.

Mallery's interests were not limited to the city of Philadelphia. Soon after the Playground Association of America was founded in 1906, he played an active role. Mallery served four years on its council, was elected to its board in 1912, and was a member the rest of his life, serving as chairman during his last six years. At the Outdoor Recreation Conference in 1924 his paper on city parks and playgrounds,

The Playground

Vol. XII No. 8	NOVEMBER 1918

Courageous Stand of Otto T. Mallery in Philadelphia

BOARD OF RECREATION

PHILADELPHIA, PA.

September 18, 1918

To the Editor:
The Playground
Cooperstown, N. Y.

Dear Sir:

The following information may interest you as a topic for your magazine. At a recent meeting of the Board of Recreation of Philadelphia, Pa., held in Room 587, City Hall, a reorganization took place. The following members were appointed and officers elected: Honorable Raymond MacNeille, Judge in the Municipal Court, President; Robert Smith, Vice-President; Edwin O. Lewis, Secretary; James A. Hamilton, Louis N. Goldsmith, authoritative writer on Athletics and member of the Board of Managers of the A. A. U. and Thomas J. Meagher, Robert Smith and James A. Hamilton were members of the incumbent Board. Judge MacNeille, Mr. Lewis, Mr. Meagher and Mr. Goldsmith were appointed by Mayor Thomas B. Smith to fill the unexpired terms of Hon. Ernest L. Tustin, Miss Sophia L. Ross and William A. Stecher.

Immediately following re-organization, the new Board elected Mr. Eduard R. Gudehus to the position of Supervisor of Recreation for the City of Philadelphia.

Very truly yours,

GENEVIEVE CARR,
In charge of Publicity

Letter to the editor on the reorganization of the Philadelphia Board of Recreation.
The Playground, November 1918

in which he stressed the need to support primary recreation needs, influenced the Conference to adopt resolution favorable to community recreation and the training of recreation leaders. Mallery's exceptional interest in the National Recreation Congress, was helpful in the preparation of Congress programs, he seldom failed to attend, and frequently served as chairman at general sessions. Few delegates enjoyed more thoroughly its play sessions and informal group activities. He was a great believer in the role of the layman in the recreation movement.

Otto Mallery hailed the Father of Recreation in Philadelphia.
Recreation, August 1944

International understanding and world peace were other causes, which Mallery supported actively. He realized that recreation was useful in attaining them. At the time the Near East Relief organization was most active, he urged them to make greater provisions for play leaders. The encouragement and assistance offered to several countries by the National Recreation Association in their efforts to establish recreation programs resulted in part from Mallery's generosity. One of the prime movers in the formation of the International Recreation Association, Mallery was a charter member of its Board of Directors.

Mallery was an outstanding layman and volunteer, he exemplified the recreation spirit, giving his time, energy, skill, and personal wealth to promote the recreation movement. At the time of his death at age 75, he was Chairman of the Board of Directors of the National Recreation Association, a Chairman Emeritus of the Philadelphia Recreation Association, and a member of the Board of the International Recreation Association. Among his most fitting tributes, Philadelphia recognized his contributions in 1956, naming one of the city's finest playgrounds in his honor and hailing him the "Father of Recreation in Philadelphia."

Adapted from:

Butler, G.D. (1965). *Pioneers in public recreation*. Minneapolis, MN: Burgess Publishing Company.
Hartsoe, C. (2007). *Building better communities: The story of the National Recreation Association (1906-1965)*. Champaign, IL: Sagamore Publishing.
National Recreation Association (August 1944). Otto Mallery, *Recreation*. 267.
National Recreation Association (August 1948). Father of Philadelphia recreation, *Recreation*. 223.
National Recreation Association (January 1957). Otto Tod Mallery, *Recreation*. 4.
Playground Association of America (November 1918). Courageous stand of Otto T. Mallery in Philadelphia. *The Playground*. 339-346.

Inducted October 1989

"*The Yosemite, the Yellowstone, the Grand Canyon are national properties in which every citizen has a vested interest; they belong as much to the man of Massachusetts, of Michigan, of Florida, as they do to the people of California, of Wyoming, and of Arizona.*"

–Stephen T. Mather

Stephen T. Mather
1867 - 1930

Born in San Francisco, Stephen Tyng Mather attended the University of California, Berkeley, before entering a short career in journalism. After working for five years as a reporter for *The New York Sun* he decided to return to his home state and assist his father in the family borax business. Mather soon earned the reputation as an advertising and promotional genius for the Thorkildsen-Mather Borax Company of Death Valley. Mather created the famous "20 Mule Team Borax" logo, making the product a virtual household name. Mather became wealthy within two decades, and by the time he was in his mid-forties, retired from the company as a millionaire.

Mather often retreated from the city to visit rural areas. He was a dedicated conservationist, a member of the Sierra Club, and friend and admirer of John Muir. On a trip through Sequoia and Yosemite National Parks in 1914, he was shocked by their conditions. Upon returning home, Mather wrote a letter to the Secretary of Interior, Franklin Lane, deploring the conditions he had found while vacationing. Lane responded with a challenge, "Dear

20 Mule Team in Death Valley.
National Park Services Historic Photograph Collection

Steve: If you don't like the way the national parks are run, why don't you come down to Washington and run them yourself?" This challenge prompted Mather to visit Washington, where Lane offered him a position to oversee the park systems. Mather accepted the position for a one year period, not realizing it would evolve into director of the National Park Service (NPS), a position he would hold for the next 14 years.

As founding director of NPS in 1916, Mather initiated a national campaign to preserve and promote the national parks and monuments. Out of his own pocket, Mather hired Robert Sterling Yard, a former colleague from *The New York Sun*, to publish the National Parks Portfolio. This publication was instrumental in creating public awareness. He also established park concessionaires to provide basic visitor comforts and services in undeveloped parks. Mather believed having the parks supported by avid users would gain the support of their elected representatives.

During Mather's administration, the NPS succeeded in enlarging some parks and adding others to the system, including Bryce Canyon, Grand Canyon, Hawaii, Lafayette (now Acadia), Lassen, Mount McKinley, and Zion. Because of his special interest in increasing parks in the East, the groundwork was laid during Mather's administration for the eventual incorporation of the Great Smoky Mountains, Shenandoah, and Mammoth Cave national parks. An additional 12 national monuments were added and the total acreage of national

Stephen Mather in side car at Yellowstone National Park, 1923.
National Park Service Historic Photograph Collection

Stephen Mather addressing delegates at the 1926 State Park Conference.
National Park Service Historic Photograph Collection

parks and monuments increased from 4,751,992 acres to 8,273, 170 acres during the Mather years.

Recognizing that not all areas qualify as national parks, Mather began discussions in 1920 to urge state governments to preserve scenic attractions and natural wonders that were of state importance. In 1921, Mather called together some 200 conservationists in Des Moines, IA, where the group "promugulated the idea of state participation in the all-American system of parks." The result of this meeting was the formation of the National Conference on State Parks, a predecessor organization to the National Recreation and Park Association. Today, the areas comprising state park systems are among the nation's outstanding and most widely used recreation resources.

Various places within today's National Park System are named after Mather, including Mather Point on the south rim of Grand Canyon National Park, Mather District in Yosemite National Park, the Mather Gorge on the border of Great Fall Park and Chesapeake and Ohio Canal National Historic Park, and the Stephen T. Mather Training Center serving the entire National Park System at Harpers Ferry National Historic Park in West Virginia. Stephen Tyng Mather High School in Chicago, IL. is also named after him, as is the Stephen Mather Memorial Parkway in the Mount Rainier National Park and the Mount Baker-Snoqualmie National Forest. In 1963 his home in Connecticut, the Stephen Tyng Mather Home, was declared a National Historic National Historic Landmark.

An outstanding park leader and influential conservationist, Stephen Mather was foremost among a group who urged Congress to set aside areas of national scenic, historic, or scientific significance and to preserve them for all time for the benefit of

Stephen Mather considered the father of the National Park System was the first Pugsley Gold Medal recipient in 1928.

all people. Millions of Americans each year enjoy the beauty and recreation afforded by the properties under the NPS, which was well established and expanded greatly under his administration. As inscribed on many plaques through the national parks in his honor, "There shall never come an end to the good he has done."

Adapted from:

Butler, G.D. (1965). *Pioneers in public recreation.* Minneapolis, MN: Burgess Publishing Company.

Crompton, J.L. (2007). *Twentieth century champions of parks and conservation: The Pugsley award recipients 1928-1964. Volume I.* Champaign, IL: Sagamore Publishing.

Ibrahim, H. (1989). *Pioneers in leisure and recreation.* Reston, VA: American Alliance for Health, Physical Education, Recreation, and Dance.

Tindall, B.S. (1971). "50 years—the origin and development of the national conference on state parks." *Parks & Recreation.* 18-20.

Inducted October 1995

"Professional groups give to people in Recreation, and those preparing to enter the field, a chance to pool their common interests for the benefit of the movement and themselves."

–Harold D. Meyer

Harold D. Meyer
1892-1974

Harold Diedrich Meyer was born in August, GA, where he received his high school education at the Academy of Richmond County, a boys' school emphasizing military training. While at the Academy, he enjoyed many extracurricular activities including the dramatics club, the glee club, and the tennis team. He was elected class president during his junior year and graduated with the honor of class valedictorian in 1908. That fall he began his social science studies at the University of Georgia. In addition to being an outstanding student, he was president of the Debator's League, president of the literary society Phi Kappa, and held memberships in the national literary fraternity Sigman Epsilon, the Dramatic Club, the University Glee Club, the Junior Cabinet, and the tennis team. Meyer graduated among the most popular and prominent of his class members, earning a Bachelor of Arts degree in 1912.

At the age of 19, Meyer entered public service as a high school principal and head football coach at Statesboro, GA. After one year, he was promoted to superintendent of schools for the 1913-1914 school year. His term as superintendent was complete in one year when he resigned and returned to the University of Georgia for graduate work in 1914. While pursuing a degree in sociology, Meyer had the good fortune of studying under the tutelage of Dr. Howard W. Odum, a nationally know sociologist. In 1915 he received his Masters of Arts degree, with a major in sociology and secured a teaching position in sociology and history in Athens, GA, at the Georgia State Normal School, an institution that later became part of the University of Georgia. Six years later he accepted a position of associate professor of sociology at the University of North Carolina, Chapel Hill.

Doctors of Recreation

The first honorary degree of *Doctor of Recreation Science* to be granted in America was awarded to Dr. Harold D. Meyer during the June commencement exercises at Salem College, Salem, West Virginia. Dr. Meyer, Professor of Sociology at the University of North Carolina and Director of the North Carolina Recreation Commission, has made many contributions to the national recreation movement. He is President of the American Recreation Society, member of the National Recreation Policies Committee, National Chairman of the Conference on State Recreation, and chairman of the College Conference on Training Recreation Leaders.

In 1944, the honorary degree of *Doctor of Recreation Service* was awarded to Dorothy Enderis at Carroll College, Waukesha, Wisconsin. The announcement regarding the bestowal of the award read, in part: "Under Dorothy Enderis's wise and far-sighted leadership, Milwaukee has developed a municipal recreation program for youths and adults that is known throughout the country for its excellence . . ."

Harold Meyer receives the first honorary degree of Doctor of Recreation Science.
Recreation, July 1948

In 1926 Meyer was promoted to professor of sociology. Concerned about society's responsibility to youth and the emergence of leisure, he developed an undergraduate curriculum in recreation within the Department of Sociology in 1932. Meyer served as chairman of the recreation curriculum from its conception in 1932 until 1963. Meyer's work in recreation education resulted in his becoming recognized as one of the foremost recreation authorities of the twentieth century. He was awarded three honorary degrees; Doctor of Laws from Florida Southern College in 1941, Doctor of Recreation Science from Salem College in 1948, and Doctor of Humanities of Learning from Catawba College in 1951. At age seventy, Meyer relinquished his position as Chairman of the recreation curriculum in 1963. He continued to teach recreation courses on a part-time basis at the University of North Carolina until 1965. After his retirement, he served as a visiting lecturer at the University of Colorado, the University of New Mexico, and Michigan State University.

Meyer was an active member of many professional organizations dedicated to the advancement of recreation: the North Carolina Recreation and Park Society; the South Carolina Recreation and Park Society; the Georgia Recreation and Park Society; the American Association of Health, Physical Education, and Recreation; the American Recreation Society; the American Institute of Park Executives; the National Industrial Recreation Association; the National Recreation Association; the International Recreation Association; and the National Recreation and Park Association. Due to his dedication in several state associations he was awarded life membership in each of the organizations. Meyer is recognized as one of the founding members of the North Carolina Recreation and Park Society,

Harold Meyer presents his recommendations to the Work Group on Leisure at the White House Conference on Aging.
American Recreation Journal, February 1961

which is recognized as one of the first state recreation agencies, established in 1944. Meyer is also acknowledged as the first person to be elected to two consecutive terms as president of the American Recreation Society and the first director of the North Carolina Recreation Commission.

Although Meyer's schedule was very busy, he found time to make a valuable contribution to recreation literature. His first major involvement was a series of twenty volumes entitled *The Extracurricular*

Library. As editor of this series between 1929 and 1935, Meyer's cumulative efforts with members of the educational field addressed such issues as finance, safety education, and student participation in school government. He joined Charles K. Brightbill to co-author four texts in recreation services including *Community Recreation: A Guide to its Organization*. This book was considered "A guide and source book for every professional recreation worker by 'front-line' author-experts." In addition to the numerous books Meyer's authored, he served on

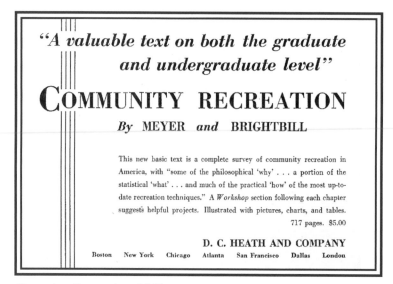

Recreation, September 1948

HAROLD D. MEYER, Re-elected

Election of Officers . . .

THE FOLLOWING OFFICERS were re-elected by the American Recreation Society at the Society's Annual Meeting, which took place at the 29th National Recreation Congress on October 16:

President, Harold D. Meyer, Chapel Hill, North Carolina; vice-president, Arthur E. Genter, Akron, Ohio; second vice-president, George T. Sargisson, Wilmington, Delaware; secretary, Wayne C. Sommer, Washington, D. C.; treasurer, Ralph Hileman, Baton Rouge, Louisiana.

Elections for Administrative Council representatives for the various geographical districts resulted in a tie in several instances. When final decisions are announced by the American Recreation Society, the list of new representatives will be published in RECREATION.

Recreation, November 1947

many editorial boards and wrote numerous articles for professional publications.

Over his career Meyer was recognized with a number of distinguishing awards. In 1962 the University of North Carolina presented him with the first Taylor L. Grandy Professor of Art and Philosophy of Living Professorship which is given to those who exemplify "the philosophy of living— teaching how to live and how to make a living." To honor his contributions, the University established the Harold D. Meyer

Award which is given annually to the most outstanding senior majoring in recreation administration. Other notable awards include the American Recreation and Park Society's Award of Merit (1969), the Society of Park and Recreation Educators' Distinguished Fellow Award (1969), and the National Recreation and Park Association's National Distinguished Professional Award(1973).

Meyer will long be remembered for his contributions to the recreation profession. His dynamic personality, his enthusiasm, his keenness as an observer, his willingness to fight for his beliefs, and his ability to analyze and interpret trends in recreation enabled him to exert a marked influence on the recreation profession. Meyer was without a doubt one of the foremost authorities on recreation in the twentieth century.

Adapted from:

North Carolina Recreation and Park Society (1974). Harold D. Meyer, 1892-1974, *North Carolina Recreation & Park Review,* Memorial Issue.
Sellers, J.R. (1971). *The contributions of Harold D. Meyer to the recreation profession.* Educat.D. dissertation, University of Georgia Retrieved May 16, 2008, from Dissertations & Theses: Full Text database. (Publication No. AAT 7211037).

Inducted October 2001

" *As long as you're fighting for parks, you can be sure of having public opinion on your side. And as long as you have public opinion on your side, you're safe.* **"**

–*Robert Moses*

Robert Moses
1888-1981

Robert Moses did more to re-shape New York City and influence the course of American urban development than any other figure of the mid-twentieth century. Neither a planner, architect, nor engineer; Moses attained unprecedented power without ever being elected to public office. In more than 30 years of public service to the city of New York and New York State, Moses achieved a reputation for building highways, parks, bridges, and recreation areas.

The son of a successful department store owner and real estate investor in New Haven, CT, Moses spent the first nine years of his life living two blocks from Yale University. Upon his father's retirement, the Moses family moved to New York City in 1897. Moses attended several preparatory schools before enrolling at Yale University. He graduated cum laude from Yale in 1909 where he was a runner, varsity swimmer, and star water polo athlete. In 1911 Moses earned his Master's degree in political science from Oxford University, England. While at Oxford he made a brilliant record

Robert Moses marker, Fordham University Lincoln Center Campus.

as a student of government and was elected to the presidency of the Oxford Union, the only American to achieve this recognition. Moses went on to obtain his doctorate degree in political science at Columbia University in New York in 1914 with a dissertation on the British civil service system.

When Alfred Smith was elected Governor of New York in 1922, he hired Moses as a speechwriter and lobbyist. Part of the reformist agenda included public parks and after convincing Governor Smith of the value and opportunities parks presented, Smith legislated to create the Long Island State Parks Commission. Moses was appointed their first president and in 1923 he mapped out a system of state parks on Long Island that would be linked together by broad parkways. The plan included appropriation of land from the estates of wealthy, influential families, who opposed his plans. Nevertheless, the plan prevailed and by 1930 Moses had built 9,700 acres of parks on Long Island. Included in this plan was the extraordinarily popular Jones Beach Park which established

Moses' national reputation when it opened in 1929. Over a quarter of a million people crowded into the park during its first month of operation to enjoy the vast beaches, enormous parking lots, campanile water tower, and its scrupulously clean boardwalk.

Moses' vision for public parks, extended far beyond the development of Long Island. As chairman of the New York Park Association's Metropolitan Conference on Parks, Moses was already planning for addition development in New York City in the late 1920s. The Metropolitan Conference issued a report in 1930 recommending immediate acquisition of thousands of acres of the last natural areas in the city. In order to solve the city's traffic problems, a system of parkways was also recommended, including the Belt, Grand Central, Cross Island, and Henry Hudson Parkways. Much of the park and parkway construction was supervised by the Parks Department which was guided by this planning report authored and sponsored by Moses.

Jones Beach Water Tower, located in Long Island State Park.

The Great Depression motivated President Franklin Delano Roosevelt to inaugurate his New Deal for the American People program in 1933. Through these federal funds Moses was able to implement his plans for the expansion of New York City's public parks through the federal Works Progress Administration. Hundreds of new facilities and venues were developed consisting of playgrounds, zoos, golf courses, and recreational buildings. Perhaps most impressive were the 11 outdoor swimming pools, with an average capacity of 5,000 people, that opened in neighborhoods throughout the city during the sweltering summer of 1936. The citizens, press, and public officials of New York City praised Moses for the development and expansion of the city's park system, gaining him appointment as New York City's parks commissioner in 1934.

By the end of World War II Moses had accumulated posts which gave him the most important single voice in park, bridge, and road construction in the New York area. Appointed New York City construction coordinator in 1946, Moses also presided over public housing and urban renewal policies, which increasingly emphasized austere high rise housing for the poor and expanded use of renewal land for private development. He had a controlling hand in many other public works projects during the 1945-1965 period, including the building of the United Nations Headquarters, Lincoln Center, the New York Coliseum, and the 1964-1965 World's Fair facilities. Moses encountered increasing opposition beginning in the late 1950s, when massive "cut and burn" urban renewal tactics began to lose favor nationally. Community opposition to his Cross Bronx Expressway (which displaced 1,500 families in a single one-mile stretch) was followed by revelations of scandals involving the misuse of urban renewal land, in which some of Moses' associates were implicated. Moses' press support had diminished by the early 1960s as, for the first time, his vision of the

Robert Moses with a model of his proposed Battery Bridge in 1939.

New York World's Fair 1964/1965 as viewed from the Observation Towers of the New York State Pavilion.
Photo by Max Mordecai

urban future seemed badly out of step with contemporary values.

Know as "the man who gets things done," Moses was the most influential non-federal public official in the nation of his time. He was an outspoken, fiery, controversial visionary whose strong character, energy, zeal, and singleness of purpose transformed the landscapes of New York State, New York City, and Long Island. He is memorialized by the Robert Moses State Park in Long Island, the Robert Moses State Park at Massena, the Robert Moses Causeway on Long Island, the Robert Moses Parkway at Niagara, and the dams at Niagara and at Massena. In 1960 Robert Moses retired as park commissioner at the age of 72. The total acreage of state parks in all 50 states at that time was 5.8 million acres. New York State had 2.6 million acres of that total, which was 45 percent of all the state park acreage in the country. Know as the "Master Builder," Moses changed shorelines, built roadways in the sky, and transformed vibrant neighborhoods forever.

Adapted from:

Caro, R.A. (1970). *The power broker: Robert Moses and the fall of New York.* New York: Alfred A. Knofp.

Crompton, J.L. (2007). *Twentieth century champions of parks and conservation: The Pugsley award recipients 1928-1964. Volume I.* Champaign, IL: Sagamore Publishing.

"The real job of an administrator is not to give orders but to inspire creative thinking in his staff... everyone is encouraged to think creatively and offer suggestions for improvement."

–William Penn Mott Jr.

Inducted October 1997

William Penn Mott Jr.
1909-1992

William Penn Mott Jr., affectionately know as Bill Mott, was born in 1909 in New York City. In 1925 he moved to Jonesville, MI, and developed an early interest for nature and the environment. Mott attended Michigan State University and earned a Bachelor's degree in landscape architecture in 1931. To expand his Midwest perspectives, he traveled west to the University of California, Berkeley, where he earned his Master's degree in landscape architecture (1933). While earning his graduate degree in "The

Golden State," Mott fell in love with the state and became one of its more decorated park and recreation professionals. Among the positions he held were superintendent of parks and recreation for Oakland, President of the Oakland Zoological Society and president of the California State Park Foundation.

For his first position, Mott was hired by the San Francisco regional office of the National Park Service to supervise landscaping duties performed by the

Civilian Conservation Corps and the Works Progress Administration (1933). In order to spend more time with his family, he took a position as a public housing planner in 1940. This enabled him to start his own landscape consulting firm. These activities resulted in his appointment as superintendent of parks for the city of Oakland. During his 17 years as superintendent, the city bloomed under his open management style. Mott's colleagues called him the man with "an idea a minute." To educate the public about the importance of protecting the environment, Mott hired Paul Covel, America's first municipal park naturalist-interpreter. It was an unheard of idea at the time, but quickly became a nationwide standard. He also created Children's Fairyland, the first three-dimensional theme park and predecessor

William Penn Mott Jr. is the only individual to receive the Cornelius Armory Pugsley Medal on three occasions: in 1972 for his work as director of the California Department of Parks and Recreation; in 1982 for his efforts as executive director of the California Parks Foundation; and in 1988 for his contributions as director of the National Park Service.
National Park Service Historic Photograph Collection

to Disneyland. By the time Mott departed Oakland to become general manager of the East Bay Regional Park District in 1962, the Oakland Parks Department gained a national reputation for excellence.

As general manager of the East Bay Regional Park District, Mott revitalized the district and helped transform it into the largest multi-county regional park system in the country. Under his guidance the East Bay Regional Park District grew from 10,500 acres to 22,000 acres and from five to 20 parks, serving a rapidly expanding population of 1.5 million in two counties. Triple the number of visitors were engaged in the park system during Mott's tenure. In 1967 Mott was appointed, by then-Governor Ronald Reagan, to serve as director of the California Department of Parks and Recreation (CDPR). During

Established on March 21, 1933 by President Franklin D. Roosevelt, the Civilian Conservation Corps were designed to combat unemployment during the Great Depression.

this time an additional 154,000 acres were added to the existing 800,000 acres of the state park system. Other acquisitions Mott started were still in progress and finalized after his departure in 1974. A total of 24 new parks, historic parks, reserves, beaches and vacation acres were added due to Mott's influence. *The California Journal* which had been leery of Mott at the beginning of his reign, by the end declared "Mott has developed a reputation as something of a magician with projects, a master manipulator of elected officials, a hard nosed negotiator for park property and a fighter to preserve the state's natural resources."

At age 65, Mott refused to retire. He became the director of park and recreation for the community of Moraga, CA. Recently established as a district, Mott said the position offered "a great challenge and opportunity to set up a prototype of a local park jurisdiction that could be copied nationwide. During this period he also provided consulting services to the East Bay Zoological Society in Oakland and was president and CEO for the California State Parks Foundation (1969-1985). Mott founded this non-profit organization while serving as State Parks director. Known for his vision, creativity, and ability as a team player, Mott was chosen by President Ronald Reagan to head the National Park Service in 1985. This position was held with distinction until Mott returned to his adopted state in 1989 to assist the Park Service in planning the Presidio's transformation from a military base to a national park. Appropriately, the visitor's center at the Presidio is named in his honor. Also bearing his name are annual awards given by the Sierra Club in park leadership and the California Department of Parks and Recreation for innovation.

William Penn Mott Jr. was a member of the Board of Trustees during the merger of the National Recreation and Park Association (1965), a charter member of the American Academy for Park and Recreation Administration (1980), and a trustee of the National Park and Conservation Association.

Mott served the park and recreation field for nearly 60 years. During his career he was a member of the Board of Trustees of the National Recreation and Park Association (1965), a charter member of the American Academy for Park and Recreation Administration (1980), and a trustee of the National Park and Conservation Association. At the time of his death in 1992, he was working primarily on plans for the transformation of the Presidio in San Francisco to its status as a National Park and assisting in the upgraded planning for Yosemite National Park. Mott was perhaps the most influential professional in the parks field of the last half of the twentieth century. His leadership in parks and recreation included service at all levels of government and several non-profit

The William Penn Mott Jr. Park Leadership Award is presented annually to a public official who demonstrates an outstanding commitment to the protection of America's natural and cultural heritage by the National Parks Conservation Association.

Photo from the cover of *Prophet of the parks: The story of William Penn Mott Jr.*

organizations and agencies. Wherever he went, programs seemed to spring to life through his inspiration and leadership. Perhaps President William Jefferson Clinton described Mott, best, calling him "one of the most vibrant and dedicated people I have ever met. He was one of a kind."

Adapted from:

American Academy of Park and Recreation Administration. (1983). *Legends of the American Park and Recreation Association* Downloaded on May 10, 2008 from http://www.aapra.org/legends.html

Butler, M.E. (1999). *Prophet of the parks: The story of William Penn Mott Jr.* Ashburn, VA: National Recreation and Park Association.

Crompton, J.L. (in press). *Twentieth century champions of parks and conservation: The Pugsley Award Recipients 1965-2007. Volume II.* Champaign, IL: Sagamore Publishing.

National Park Service, directors of the National park Service, Downloaded on May 14, 2008 from http://www.nps.gov/history/history/hisnps/NPSHistory/directors.html

Inducted October 1988

"The beauty of the park...should be of the fields, the meadow, the prairie, of the green pastures, and the still waters. What we want to gain is tranquility and rest to the mind.""

–Frederick Law Olmsted

Frederick Law Olmsted
1822-1903

Born to a prosperous merchant in Hartford, CT, Frederick Law Olmsted acquired a youthful interest in people and their environment. Due to a vision problem caused by sumac poisoning, Olmsted's plan to attend Yale College in 1837 was altered. Early occupations as a seaman, merchant, and journalist influenced his perspectives. As a journalist, he visited Birkenhead Park in Merseyside, England in 1850. This trip inspired him to write *Walks and Talks of an American Farmer in England* (1852). In this publication, he commented about Birkenhead Park:

"Five minutes of admiration, and a few more spent studying the manner in which art had been employed to obtain from nature so much beauty, and I was ready to admit that in democratic America there was nothing to be thought of as comparable with this People's Garden."

Perhaps this inspiration affected the way America looks. Olmsted is best known as the creator of major urban parks across the nation, from green spaces that help define our towns and cities, to suburban life, to protected wilderness areas, he left the imprint of his fertile mind and boundless energy. Out of his deep love for the land and his social commitment, he fathered the profession of landscape architecture in America.

The Boathouse at Birkenhead Park, England. Photo by S.F. Barnes

Regarded as a key figure in the American park movement, Olmsted's influence was vital in establishing parks throughout the nation. As Central Park's first superintendent, he, along with Calvert Vaux, conceived the Greensward Plan, the award winning design that guided the development of Central Park. The success of their innovative park design created a demand for Olmsted's services in other cities. Over the years, the landscape architecture firm he established developed plans for 650 public park and recreation areas.

Frederick Law Olmsted
Oil painting by John Singer Sargent, 1895

Olmsted's foresight led to the development of urban environmental areas open to use by all people. He believed the purpose for the creation of Central Park was "to be that of permanently affording, in the densely populated central portion of an immense metropolis, a means to certain kinds of refreshment of the mind and nerves which most city dwellers greatly need and which they are known to derive in large measure from the enjoyment of suitable scenery." He was convinced his work could influence society. The parks Olmsted planned were to be spaces common to all residents of the cities, where all types of people could mingle free from the harsh influences of urban life. He believed that scenery had a profound psychological effect on people and that the open and natural terrain of parks provided a specific medical antidote to the stresses of city life. To Olmsted, parks promoted a sense of community through accessibility to the poor as well as the rich.

In addition to Central Park, Olmsted also designed Riverside and Morningside Parks in New York City; South Park and Jackson Park in Chicago; the Boston Park System; Belle Island in Detroit; and parks in Albany, Buffalo, Rochester, San Francisco, Newark, Philadelphia, Hartford, Trenton, Louisville, Milwaukee and Kansas City, among others.

Adapted from:

National Park Service Brochure on the Frederick Law Olmsted National Historic Site.

Central Park, The Mall
Photo by Patricia Heintzelman, Historic Sites Survey, National Park Service, Washington, D.C.

Central Park, Pilgram Hill
Photo by Patricia Heintzelman, Historic Sites Survey, National Park Service, Washington, D.C.

Inducted October 1988

George A. Parker
1853 - 1926

Born a country boy in Fitzwilliam, NH, George Amos Parker attended a "country school" until the age of 11 or 12. During his teenage years, he worked at a country store, area farm, and chair factory. At age 19, he had saved enough money to enroll in classes at the Massachusetts Agricultural College in Amherst. In 1876, he graduated and pursued a career in landscape architecture, with his first professional job as head gardener at Vassar College, New York. Over the next two decades, Parker held landscaping, planning, and development appointments for public and private estates throughout the Midwest and New England area, including the famous summer home "Gray Gables," of President Grover Cleveland.

Parker was hired in 1896 as superintendent of Keney Park in Hartford, Connecticut. Superseded by Theodore Wirth, he was appointed in 1906 as Hartford's superintendent of parks and served until his retirement in 1926. Parker developed one of the finest park systems of his time, believing that city parks could

Tenth Tee at Keney Park Golf, May 1937.
Hartford History Center, Hartford Public Library

First Municipal Rose Garden in Elizabeth Park, early 1900s.
Hartford History Center, Hartford Public Library

The New England Association of Park Superintendents

An excerpt from a letter Theodore Wirth wrote his son Walter L. Wirth on December 18, 1934.

It was a blizzard March day in 1898 when George A. Parker, Superintendent of Keney Park, walked into my office in Bushnell Park and asked me, "How many park superintendents are you acquainted with?" After a minute I said, "None but Samuel Parsons of New York and yourself." He then asked, "Would you be willing to join an organization of park officials of the New England States?" To which I answered that I most certainly would be glad to do so.

Mr. Parker consulted a few more park men and, on the invitation of J.A. Pettigrew, whom he knew, issued a call for a meeting at the Brunswick Hotel in Boston, April 6-7, 1898. At this meeting the following were present:

1.	Jackson Dawson	Superintendent Arnold Arboretum	Boston Mass.
2.	J.A. Pettigrew	Superintendent of Parks	Boston, Mass.
3.	Jas. B. Shea	Ass't Superintendent of Parks	Boston, Mass.
4.	Robert Elder	Superintendent, Beaver Brook Res.	Waverly, Mass.
5.	Frank Dings	Superintendent, Blue Hills Res.	Milton, Mass.
6.	H.H. Williams	Superintendent, Hemlock Gorge Res.	Upper Falls, Mass.
7.	Chas P. Price	Superintendent, Middlesex Falls	Melrose, Mass.
8.	H.W. West	Superintendent, Revere Beach Res.	Crescent Beach, Mass.
9.	H.S. Adams	Superintendent of Parks	Arlington, Mass.
10.	B.R. Chapman	Superintendent of Parks	Brockton, Mass.
11.	E.W. Bailey	Superintendent of Parks	Somerville, Mass.
12.	Chas. S. Anthony	Superintendent of Parks	Taunton, Mass.
13.	Chas. F. Lawton	Superintendent of Parks	New Bedford, Mass.
14.	J.A. Holmes	Superintendent of Parks	Cambridge, Mass.
15.	H.A. Hastings	Superintendent of Parks	Springfield, Mass.
16.	Henry Frost	Superintendent of Parks	Haverill, Mass.
17.	Joseph D. Fitts	Superintendent of Parks	Providence, R.I.
18.	Theodore Wirth	Superintendent of Parks	Hartford, Conn.
19.	Chas. E. Keith	Superintendent of Parks	Bridgeport, Conn.
20.	Geo. A. Parker	Superintendent of Keney Park	Hartford, Conn.
21.	Walter Hubbard	Superintendent, Hubbard Parks	Meriden, Conn.
22.	John C. Olmsted	Landscape Architect	Brookline, Mass.
23.	Wm. J. Steward	Secretary, Society American Florists	Boston, Mass.
24.	Frederick Harris	Superintendent of Parks	Wellesley, Mass.
25.	Jos. R. Carr	Secretary, Park Board	Chelsea, Mass.
26.	William Doogue	Superintendent, Public Gardens	Boston, Mass.

From the meager records at my disposal, it would seem that Mr. Hemingway was not at the meeting of organization, but was nevertheless later elected as Treasurer.

A banquet was held at the Brunswick Hotel the evening of April 6, at which a committee was appointed to draft a constitution and bylaws, consisting of Messrs. J.A. Pettigrew, Jackson Dawson, Joseph Fitts, William Doogue, and George A. Parker. This draft was sent to every member and was presented at the next meeting for consideration and adoption.

The second day an inspection trip of the Boston and Cambridge parks was made as guests of the park authorities of the two cities, which proved to be very instructive. At the close of that first meeting and inspection trip, Charles Keith of Bridgeport made the following pertinent remarks – "I went to Boston feeling that I have gained twenty-five friends" – and so we felt, all of us.

George Amos Parker was the originator of the idea and the real founder of our organization, and it behooves us to respect and honor his memory as such for all times to come.

National Recreation and Park Association (July 1, 1998). As ever yours, Dad.
Parks & Recreation, Centennial Celebration Issue

Foax Bridge in Keney Park, early 1900s.
Hartford History Center, Hartford Public Library

He furthermore believed that parks provided households a place to socialize within their communities. Hartford's park system is recognized for creating the first municipal rose garden in the world (1903) and for its early development of a municipal golf course, attractive facilities, game courts, and playfields.

While working in Hartford, Parker sensed the lack of opportunity for professional fellowship in the newly emerging park field. Parker helped organize a group of park superintendents in the New England region to form the first professional organization in the park and recreation field. The group's initial meeting was in 1898 and from this meeting, the New England Association of Park Superintendents came into existence. This early organization evolved into the American Institute of Park Executives (AIPE), which guided the park movement in America until 1965. That year, AIPE joined with four other national organizations to form the National Recreation and Park Association.

Parker poured his own money into publishing and distributing the association's bulletins. He encouraged his fellow members to write and share their knowledge and experience with one another. These early bulletins were the beginning of what is now *Parks and Recreation* magazine.

During an interview in 1906, he stated, "I have visited more than 1,400 parks in the United States, and am acquainted with their history." At the time there were only 3,500 parks in the country. Distinguished as one of the foremost nineteenth century park executives; Parker's vision and foresight helped develop and enhance the park profession. He may have been known as one of the great networkers of the field.

Adapted from:

Alderman adopt minutes on death of G.A. Parker. (1927, February 15). *The Hartford Courant.*
Baldwin, P.C. (1997). Off the street: Reforming the use of public space in Hartford, 1850-1930. Unpublished master's thesis, Brown University, Providence, RI.
Butler, G.D. (1965). *Pioneers in public recreation.* Minneapolis, MN: Burgess Publishing Company.
First vacation in forty years. (1919, July 16). *The Hartford Courant.* 20.
National Recreation and Park Association (July 1, 1998). "As ever yours, dad." *Parks & Recreation,* Centennial Celebration Issue.

Inducted October 1999

"One of the great values of the National Recreation Association is its bringing together in a single organization both professional recreation leaders and citizens interested in the development of the recreation movement."

–Joseph Prendergast

Joseph Prendergast
1904-1992

A lawyer and social welfare administrator, Joseph Prendergast replaced Howard Brancher as executive director of the National Recreation Association (NRA). He served from 1950 through the merger that created the National Recreation and Park Association.

A native of Chicago, Prendergast attended Exeter Academy in New Hampshire and graduated from Princeton in 1927. He is the only student in the history of the university to be elected president of his class each of his four undergraduate years. He was co-founder of the National Student Federation of America, the first student organization ever formed, and was president of the Cap and Gown Club.

Prendergast was a star half-back (Five Yard Prendergast) on the 1925 and 1926 Princeton football teams, where he made second team All-American. After graduating from Princeton, he studied law at Balliol College, Oxford University on a scholarship.

Princeton Football Team, 1916. From left top row: Requardt, Howe, Willauer, Miles, Stinson, Baruch, and Bridges. From left second row: Collins (Mgr), Chandler, French, Rosengarten, Ewing, Prendergast, William, Keith, and Fitzpatrick. From left bottom row: Balwin, Darby, Moeser, Davis (Capt.), Slagle, Caulkins, and Batell.
Princeton University Library

In 1935 he was named Assistant U.S. Attorney for the Southern district of New York, later holding top jobs in the Department of Justice in Washington. Enlisting in the U.S. Army as a private in 1942, he rose to the rank of major and was wounded and taken prisoner by the Germans near the Rhine, escaped, recovered, and received numerous combat decorations.

During his recuperation period in a military hospital, he decided to focus his career in social service. Following the war, he received a Master's of Science degree from Columbia University's School of Social Work, specializing in social action and community organization. Always interested in youth sports and those underserved, he worked after the war in social welfare until his appointment to executive director of the National Recreation Association.

Prendergast was successful in strengthening NRA's financial base and in expanding the Association's traditional services, such as the magazine, annual conference, field services, and publications. In addition, he established an international recreation service (the forerunner to the World Leisure and Recreation Association) and a new consulting service in recreation for the ill and handicapped.

On the 50th Anniversary of the NRA, Prendergast was instrumental in purchasing the Whitney Museum of American Art at 8 West 8th St. in New York City as the new headquarters for the National Recreation Association.

Prendergast's professional involvements were extensive. President Eisenhower appointed him to the National Citizen's Advisory Committee on Fitness of American Youth in 1957. He was the first chairman of the National Advisory Council to Keep America Beautiful, Inc., and Vice-chairman of the Citizens' Committee of the National Advisory Council to the Outdoor Recreation Resources Review Commission. He was a member of the

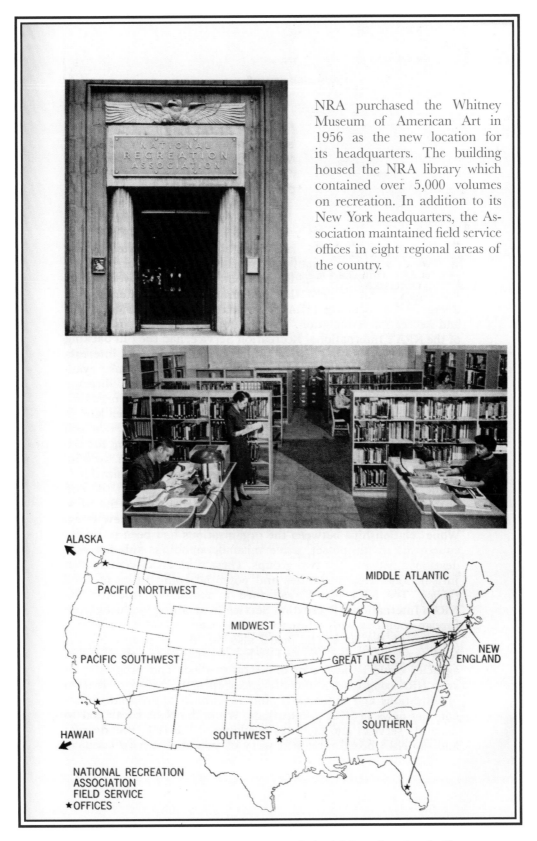

NRA purchased the Whitney Museum of American Art in 1956 as the new location for its headquarters. The building housed the NRA library which contained over 5,000 volumes on recreation. In addition to its New York headquarters, the Association maintained field service offices in eight regional areas of the country.

ALASKA

PACIFIC NORTHWEST

MIDDLE ATLANTIC

MIDWEST

PACIFIC SOUTHWEST

GREAT LAKES

NEW ENGLAND

HAWAII

SOUTHWEST

SOUTHERN

NATIONAL RECREATION
ASSOCIATION
FIELD SERVICE
★ OFFICES

(Top) NRA headquarters building, (middle) NRA library, (below) Map of regional offices.
Play for America, 1979

ARS/NRA officials meet in New York in January 24, 1962, to discuss how the combined strength of both organizations could be used most effectively for the good of the national recreation movement and the interest of the people it serves. From left: Joseph Prendergast, Executive Director, National Recreation Association; James H. Evans, Chairman of the Board, National Recreation Association; William Frederickson Jr., President, American Recreation Society; and Ray Butler, Executive Director of the ARS.
American Recreation Journal, Frebruary 1962

National Advisory Committee to the 1961 White House Conference on Aging and served on the board of directors of the Police Athletic League of New York City. Among his international involvements were membership in the United States Olympic Committee (1966-1967) and the Executive Foreign Relations Committee of the Amateur Athletic Union of America (1964-1967).

Prendergast was a major force in promoting the concept of citizen and professional cooperation. He believed that parks and recreation was strengthened through the unity of these two major elements, that with citizen input and support, tempered with professional understanding and technique, the public's park and recreation interests would be best met.

In 1955 Springfield College, MA awarded an honorary degree of Doctor of Law to Prendergast for his service to the national recreation movement. In 1964 Prendergast was instrumental in the creation of the National Recreation Foundation, an independent grant-making non-profit corporation. His role in the creation of the National Recreation Park

and Association and the leadership he gave that organization in its formative years are testaments to his leadership and commitment.

Prendergast believed in the importance of preserving historical artifacts and buildings. He assumed responsibility as executive director of the National Trust for Historic Preservation in the United States in 1967 and served in that capacity until his retirement in 1973. At the time of his death he resided at Oak Hill Farm in Aldie, VA, in a house designed by Thomas Jefferson and occupied by James Monroe when he wrote the Monroe Doctrine.

Adapted from:

American Academy of Park and Recreation Administration. (1983). *Legends of the American Park and Recreation Association* Downloaded on May 10, 2008 from http://www.aapra.org/legends.html

Knapp, R. and Hartsoe, C. (1979). *Play for America*. Ashburn, VA: National Recreation and Park Association.

Material from Daniel J. Link. Princeton University Archivist.

National Recreation Association (February, 1950). Joseph Prendergast new executive director, *Recreation*. 511.

Inducted October 1991

" Those who are happily occupied in wholesome leisure time pursuits will never become problems to their community either as children or as adults. "

–Josephine D. Randall

Josephine D. Randall
1885-1975

One of the first women in America to choose recreation leadership as a profession, Josephine Randall achieved a long and distinguished career. A native of California, she attended Stanford University where she earned an undergraduate degree (1909), a graduate degree (1910), and was a member of Sigma Chi Honorary Scientific Research Fraternity. While completing her Master's degree in zoology, she developed a philosophy for "the good life." Upon graduation, Randall chose a career in recreation to provide guidance and leadership for people to do things for the express purpose of finding pleasure in doing them.

In 1913 Randall became the first woman director to be appointed to San Diego's public playgrounds. Her main concern was for the children of the community, but did not exclude the needs of adults. During her six year appointment, she also organized one of the first Girl Scout troops in America, one of the early Campfire groups, and during World War I worked with the War Camp Community Service. She was a firm believer that recreation provides an opportunity to "re-create one's self" thus finding renewed energies and happiness in meeting the everyday problems of the world.

Randall joined the staff of the National Recreation Association in 1920 and served for four years as field representative in the Middle West and Pacific Coast. In her work with the Association she demonstrated a comprehensive knowledge of the field of recreation, unusual organizing ability, and a special aptitude for training recreation leaders. As a field representative, Randall became aware of San Francisco's lack of recreation facilities in 1924, when she began a community chest survey of the city's needs. She also organized the Group Work and Recreation Council of the Community Chest. After completion of this work, she was employed as Superintendent of the San Francisco Recreation Department, where she served from 1926 until 1951.

During the quarter century Randall was executive, the San Francisco Recreation Department developed one of the country's

Boys from the Chinese Playground in San Francisco exhibit intricate kites.
Recreation, November 1943

outstanding community recreation services. Drama groups were organized at each of the city's recreation centers. Augustus Zanzig, in his book, *Music in American Life* (1932), highly praised the department's music program. It included a glee club of Italian boys, a boys' harmonica club, girls' glee clubs, and a group of singing mothers. Under her guidance, the Recreation Department grew from 22 playgrounds to over 100 recreation units including a city vacation camp, children's day camps, a photography center, and the Junior Museum.

Randall's innovative plan for assigning workers in neighborhoods of the heaviest delinquency, inaugurated in 1930 by the San Francisco Recreation Department, proved to be one of the most successful services. Workers came to know the people in their district, particularly the gangs. They became familiar with the functions and resources of the neighborhood agencies, and referred boys to the various public and private recreation centers in their vicinity. There were striking results in the reduction of juvenile delinquency, youth crime, and

Literal translation of the five Chinese characters, reading from right to left is: "Chinese," "People," "Recreation," "Leisure," and "Field," which, when put together add up to a Chinese playground.
Recreation, October 1942

Harmonica Band at the Chinese Playground, San Francisco.
An Album of Programs in the Early Years of Public Recreation

in the rehabilitation of troubled boys. A Central Coordinating Council partnering Randall, the chief of Police, the chief probation officer, and the superintendent of schools was set up to guide the plan and was an important factor in its success.

Under Randall's leadership one of America's most extensive and successful recreation programs in public housing developments was established. In 1941 through the cooperation of the San Francisco Housing Authority, the Recreation Department accepted responsibility for furnishing leadership in local housing developments. By 1945 the department operated 16 centers, many of them serving workers in war industries. Leadership was provided at least 12 hours per day and seven days a week in most centers. The program was of vital importance to the thousands of newcomers to the city, to the Japanese-Americans who returned to their home

city from relocation centers, and to refugee families liberated in the Philippines. The Housing Authority increasingly enlisted the cooperation of the department in the planning of its recreation facilities was evidence of its success in dealing with these complex and acute problems and testified to the capability of Randall and her staff.

Inspired by the ideals of the United Nations' Educational, Scientific, and Cultural Organizations, Randall developed a deep interest in the people of other nations and in the international aspects of recreation. Members of many nationality groups participated without discrimination in the recreation program of the city, which was a veritable melting pot. She brought to the people of San Francisco an understanding of other nations through the presentation of special programs built around their games, arts and crafts, customs, dances, songs, and folklore. After

Randall has the distinction of being the first woman to receive a citation naming her as a Fellow of the American Recreation Society. In 1948 she received an honorary Doctorate from the University of California.
ReCreation Bulletin, 1949

she retired as superintendent of recreation, Randall spent a year touring Europe as a goodwill ambassador representing the California Recreation Society.

It was Randall's dream to create "a spot in the heart of the city where young people could spend a day in the country." In 1937 her vision came to fruition. Simply called the "Junior Museum," it originally opened in the city's old jail on Ocean Avenue. Randall shepherded a $12,000,000 bond issue for recreation capital projects in 1947 which including a new museum. The museum opened in 1951 at its current facilities on a 16-acre park overlooking San Francisco Bay and was renamed the Josephine D. Randall Junior Museum, later renamed Randall Museum. The life's work of Randall remains monumental. Her visionary efforts in addressing the needs of urban youth and the melting pot of different cultures are an example of the value recreation contributes to communities.

Adapted from:

Butler, G.D. (1965). *Pioneers in public recreation*. Minneapolis, MN: Burgess Publishing Company.

National Recreation Association (November 1951). After thirty-eight years of service, *Recreation*. 348.

National Recreation Association (April, 1957). A reporter's notebook, *Recreation*. 132.

San Francisco Recreation Department (February 14, 1949). Our superintendent awarded American recreation fellowship, *ReCreation Bulletin*, 17(7). 4.

"You are not just playing games or participating in events. You are helping to build nations. You are helping to build peace. You are helping to build the kind of world to which leisure, in freedom prevails."

–Thomas E. Rivers

Inducted October 1997

Thomas E. Rivers
1892-1977

Thomas Ellis Rivers' career in recreation spanned a period of approximately 60 years. While recognized as a national leader during the formative years of the recreation movement, Rivers' principal influence was the development of recreation and leisure services on an international level. He was one of the leading forces in the creation of the International Recreation Association in 1956, later to be renamed the World Leisure and Recreation Association.

Rivers was born on October 6, 1892, in Meridan, MI. Upon graduation from Mount Hermon Preparatory School in Northfield, MA, he enrolled at the University of Wisconsin, where he pursued an undergraduate program in social sciences. At the time Rivers graduated, World War I was still in progress. Shortly after receiving his degree, Rivers was inducted into the Army and assigned to a newly created civilian agency whose mission was to help local communities provide leisure activities for military personnel in communities and away from the military bases. War Camp

Thomas Rivers was awarded an honorary Doctor of Humanities degree from Springfield College, MA, in recognition for his work in recreation and leisure at the international level.
American Recreation Journal, October 1960

Community Services (WCCS) was an organization created by the Playground and Recreation Association to deal with the unprecedented leisure needs of a newly mobilized national military force. It was this early experience in dealing with the leisure needs of military personnel that helped shape Rivers' lifelong career.

Following World War I, Rivers remained on the staff of an expanded National Recreation Association, predecessor of the WCCS. Over the succeeding years, he held a number of prominent national staff positions, including that of a southern field representative, manager of personnel and placement services, secretary of the National Recreation School, and secretary of the National Recreation Congress, a position which he held for over 30 years. While on the staff of the National Recreation Association (NRA), Rivers developed a reputation as one of the most effective fund raisers for recreation in the nation.

Rivers' interest in international recreation was stimulated by his responsibility for planning the first International Recreation Congress, held in Los Angeles, preceding the 1932 Olympic Games. This congress, hosted by the NRA, attracted more than 100 delegates from 40 countries. The success of this meeting prompted plans for a second international meeting to coincide with the 1936 Berlin Olympics. However, the potential for Adolph Hitler to expand Nazi propaganda through the Olympic process caused the NRA to boycott the second international meeting and it was not until 1956 that another major international meeting on recreation and leisure would be held.

Shah of Iran receives gold medal and certificate from T.E. Rivers, executive secretary, International Recreation Service.
Recreation, February 1956

Thomas Rivers addresses members of the international advisory committee at IRA's organizational meeting in October 1956.
WLRA Journal, January/February 1981

During the 1950s, Rivers was instrumental in establishing a new International Recreation Service within the structure of the National Recreation Association. The development of this new service was stimulated by an extensive worldwide trip made by Rivers and his wife, Ruth, in 1952. During this trip, Rivers made contact with recreation leaders and public

Mr. and Mrs. Rivers and Vice-Admiral Norman, general secretary, National Playing Fields Association, at Buckingham Palace after seeing Duke of Edinburgh.
Recreation, March 1956

officials in several countries, including Italy, Spain, Portugal, Greece, Egypt, Jordan, Lebanon, Pakistan, India, Thailand, Philippines, Hong Kong, and Japan. While in Japan, he presented medals and citations from the NRA to several Japanese recreation leaders and represented NRA at the sixth Japanese Recreation Congress. This trip made it clear of the exceptional opportunity for development of recreation and leisure on an international scale. In September 1953 the NRA established an office in Carnegie Endowment International Center to house the International Recreation Services. This office, headed by Rivers, was directly across from the United Nations in New York City.

Rivers was soon to develop a reputation as the "global ambassador of recreation." In 1955 he undertook a second major international journey, which took him to 22 countries where he met with both professional, and citizen leaders interested in recreation. This visit, along with his 1952 international trip, helped lay the groundwork for organizing the 1956 International Recreation Congress held in Philadelphia. This congress commemorated the golden anniversary of the NRA, and also served to launch the creation of the

345 EAST 46th STREET, UNITED NATIONS PLAZA
NEW YORK, N.Y. 10017
(212) 697-8783   CABLE • RECREATE, NEW YORK

CHARTER FOR LEISURE
Prologue

All societies and all cultures increasingly recognise people's right to certain periods of time during which they can choose freely how to occupy themselves and which experiences to select to further their quest for self-fulfillment and to improve the quality of their lives.

Peace, a minimum of social stability, the opportunity to establish meaningful inter-personal contacts, and the reduction of social inequality are some of the major prerequisites for the full implementation of that right.

Although the word *leisure* has different meanings in different parts of the world and although it is unknown in a large number of languages, all cultures and all language groups have, within their vocabularies, words referring to those functions that are usually associated with the concept of leisure.

Therefore, for the purposes of this charter, leisure is seen as the equivalent of concepts such as "Freizeit," "Tiempo Libre," "Vryetydsbesteding," "Loisir," "Lazer" and others.

Freedom and choice are its central elements; freedom to develop one's talents, to pursue one's interests, to improve the quality of one's life; choice from amongst a large variety of opportunities, thus expanding one's options and range of experiences.

Recreation in this context is seen as a personal response to fulfilling, regenerative and enjoyable activities that can be engaged in during free time.

Article 1

Leisure is a basic human right. This implies the obligation of governments to recognise and protect this right and of citizens to respect the right of fellow citizens to leisure.

This means that no one shall be deprived of this right for reasons of colour, creed, sex, religion, race, handicap or economic condition.

Article 2

Recreation is a social service of similar importance as Health and Education.

Therefore, opportunities must be provided on a universal basis, reasonable access ensured, and appropriate variety and quality maintained.

Article 3

Ultimately, the individual person is his/her own best leisure and recreation resource; the primary roles of governments, private agencies and groups are of a supporting nature, consisting of the provision of services where needed, with prime emphasis at the local level.

Article 4

Leisure and recreation opportunities should stress self-fulfillment, the development of interpersonal relationships, the fostering of family and social integration, international understanding and cooperation, and the strengthening of cultural identities.

Special emphasis must be placed on maintaining the quality of the environment and on the influence of energy demands on future recreation resources.

Article 5

The development of recreation leaders, animators and/or counsellors must be undertaken wherever possible. The main tasks of these must include assisting people in discovering and developing their talents and helping them acquire desired personal skills for the purpose of broadening the range of recreation opportunities.

Article 6

The wide variety of leisure and recreation phenomena, including personal and collective experiences, must be subjected to systematic research and scholarly inquiry, with results being disseminated as widely as possible to enhance the individual's knowledge of him/herself, to provide a stronger rationale for policy decisions, and to provide a more effective basis for program development and operation.

All citizens must have access to all forms of information relative to the various aspects of leisure and recreation.

Article 7

Educational institutions at all levels must place special emphasis on the teaching of the importance of leisure and recreation, on helping students discover their leisure and recreation potential and on ways to integrate leisure and recreation into their lifestyles.

These institutions should furthermore provide appropriate opportunities from which recreation leaders and educators can be developed.

Epilogue

The present charter is the result of a thorough review process of the "Charter of Leisure" as it was adopted by the Internationl Recreation Association in May, 1970, Geneva, Switzerland. This review was initiated at a workshop held during the Second International Conference on Recreation and Leisure Leadership Development in San Juan, Puerto Rico, October 22-26, 1979.

Subsequent to this, a draft charter was prepared on the basis of which the views of a large number of individuals and agencies from around the world were sought, culminating in significant input obtained from the participants in the study sessions that took place in Twannberg, Switzerland, from November 5-11, 1981 at the occasion of the World Leisure and Recreation Association's 25th Annual General Meeting.

The views and opinions thus acquired formed the basis of yet another concept charter which, after having been scrutinized by the participants in the Puerto Rico Workshop and the WLRA Board of Directors, resulted in the present adopted version.

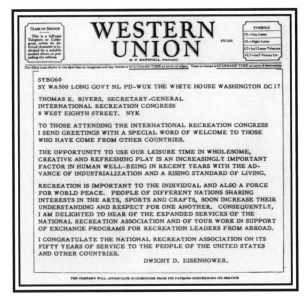

Western Union gram from President Dwight D. Eisenhower welcoming delegates of the International Recreation Congress, Philadelphia, 1956.
National Recreation and Park Association Archives

International Recreation Association. Rivers was appointed director general of the new organization, a position he held for 18 years. Under Rivers' leadership, the International Recreation Association quickly established worldwide identity. Within three years, they became financially independent and no longer required budgetary support from the NRA.

Many accomplishments stand out during Rivers' 18 years as director general. Among his most significant accomplishments were helping to organize national recreation associations in Brazil, Pakistan, India, Korea, Columbia, and Israel; providing leadership for the 1964 World Congress which took place in Japan; assisting in the formation of the European Recreation and Leisure Association and providing an expanded international philosophy. This broadened philosophy was evidence by an organizational name change in 1973 from International Recreation Association to World Leisure and Recreation Association.

A testimonial to Rivers' philosophy and leadership was the creation of a worldwide Charter of Leisure. This document, developed over a two and half-year period by an International Recreation Association committee, became an important tool for furthering recreation and leisure on a worldwide basis. It is evidence of Rivers' vision of "Building a Better World through Recreation."

Adapted from:

Butler, G.D. (1965). *Pioneers in public recreation.* Minneapolis, MN: Burgess Publishing Company.

Ibrahim, H. (1989). *Pioneers in leisure and recreation.* Reston, VA: American Alliance for Health, Physical Education, Recreation and Dance.

National Recreation Association (September, 1955). World service through recreation, *Recreation.* 320-321.

National Recreation Association (January, 1957). The launching of the International Recreation Association, *Recreation.* 12-13.

Inducted October 2003

"The story of the recreation movement will not be one of organizational charts, constitutions, structure, and committees; rather, it will be the story of its leadership."

–Willard C. Sutherland

Willard C. Sutherland
1902-1994

In June 1927, an A.B. degree in his hand, Willard Sutherland graduated from Drake University in Des Moines, IA, where he had made a name for himself as a student and an athlete. His interest in recreation was made evident by the fact that, in October of that same year, he applied for enrollment in the National Recreation School and was accepted. The school, then in its second year, conducted an intensive one-year graduate course designed to develop broad executive leadership for the recreation movement.

Upon graduating from the National Recreation School in May 1928 as one of the top ranked students in his class, he was employed by the National Recreation Association (NRA) beginning on July 1, 1928. His professional contributions to the recreation movement were made through the National Recreation Association and its successor, the National Recreation and Park Association for more than 40 years.

In his earlier years with the NRA, Sutherland was in the field promoting organized recreation in numerous

RECREATION
AS A PROFESSION
IN THE SOUTHERN REGION

Report of a Joint Study
by
The National Recreation Association
and
The Southern Regional Education Board
1952 - 1954

a Publication of the
NATIONAL RECREATION ASSOCIATION
A Service Organization Supported by Voluntary Contributions
8 West Eighth Street   New York 11, N. Y.

One of Sutherland's publications through the National Recreation Association.

communities and assisting with the work of the Field Department at the national NRA headquarters. It was not long, however, until his aptitude for personnel work became apparent. In 1934, this led to his assignment as director to the Association's Recreation Personnel Service.

With his leadership, the NRA developed a comprehensive personnel system that included a national registration program, a placement service, an expansion of regional and national training programs, and a cooperative national internship program between the Association and some of the premier local recreation and park departments. Sutherland, called "Woody" by friends and colleagues, participated in an extensive college visitation program where he met with recreation and park faculty and students.

He also played an important role in elevating the status of recreation as a profession. He was instrumental in having recreation mentioned as a career in the College Placement Annual, the Peace Corps Occupational Manual, and the Directory of Occupational Titles.

By 1963 some 13,000 personnel records (both active and inactive) were on file with the NRA. In that same year, the NRA's Personnel Service received over 9,000 communications related to personnel services which resulted in over 17,000 outgoing communications. This included 6,000 notices to candidates about over 400 position vacancies. It also included 964 sets of formal confidential personnel records sent to employers on request.

Sutherland edited a monthly column in *Recreation* magazine on personnel matters. In addition, he authored several publications on the recruitment and training of recreation personnel. He also conducted a major study on "Recreation as a Profession in the Southern Region."

He established the very successful annual National Institute in Recreation Administration, which was held in conjunction with the National Congress. The institute was always over-subscribed. From 1928 through 1969, Sutherland was centrally involved in establishing university curricula and developing training programs. He played a major role in formulating the recreation and park profession as we know it today.

In an interview prior to his retirement, his thoughts about the profession he served so well were recorded and bear repeating: On the NRPA:
"The inherent power of the merger of park, recreation, and conservation agencies

Sutherland established a national internship program in cooperation with several recreation and park departments across the nation. NRPA past-president, Robert Toalson was among the first to complete this program. Toalson is seen receiving his certificate of achievement, from Philadelphia's recreation commissioner, Robert Crawford. Toalson went on to serve as president as both National Recreation and Park Association and American Academy for Parks and Recreation Administration. *Building Better Communities*

has given the Association the greatest potential for good of any organization."

On advising today's graduates:

"The young graduate should be sure that he has a belief, not just an interest in the profession. If he has a commitment and is oriented toward growth, spiritual stature and opportunity for service, he need never worry about security."

On the Park and Recreation leadership:

"The story of the recreation movement will not be one of organizational charts, constitutions, structure, and committees; rather, it will be the story of its leadership."

"The leader of the future will have a highly developed personal philosophy of life and a well thought out philosophy of leisure. He will be steeped in the behavioral sciences."

"Leadership in quality and quantity is our number one problem. The profession that does not recruit its own is doomed to mediocrity at best."

"I believe that the most important

Last graduating class of the NRA School, 1935. The school was established in 1926 for professional training. Among the top ranked students in the class of 1928, Sutherland gained employment upon graduation with the National Recreation Association in July of 1928.
National Recreation and Park Association Archives

responsibility of an executive is the development of people. All that we accomplish, all that we get done is through people."

In his retirement in Florida, Sutherland gave countless volunteer hours to the American Red Cross, to the Presbyterian Church, and to local hospitals. He was the ultimate volunteer even to his 90th year.

Adapted from:

American Academy of Park and Recreation Administration. (1983). *Legends of the American Park and Recreation Association* Downloaded on May 10, 2008 from http://www.aapra.org/legends.html
National Recreation Association. (October 1952). Person. *Recreation.* 294.
National Recreation Association. (June, 1956). Development and growth of a profession. *Recreation.* 300-302.
National Recreation Association. (July, 1968). This is your National Recreation Association, *Parks & Recreation.* 35 & 50.

Inducted October 2005

"Where everybody is somebody."
–Grambling State University Motto

Pearl H. Vaughn
1914-1986

Pearl H. Vaughn, an innovative educator and community recreation leader, was a true trailblazer. As an African-American female, she was at the forefront, promulgating the love of her chosen profession with deeds and actions unusual for a woman of color in the middle decade of the 20th century.

Vaughn was born in Chattanooga, TN, graduated from Tennessee State University, and began her career as a recreation leader. Later, she served as a supervisor for the Memphis Department of Parks and Recreation. In 1962 she accepted a faculty position at Grambling State University.

Grambling State University, steeped in history and a long-standing tradition of excellence, was the first historically black college or university to achieve accreditation in both physical education and recreation. Through the years, the university has acquired the prestige and academic strength noted only among much larger institutions. It is one of the country's top producers of African-American graduates.

Students leaving for a trip to the National Recreation and Park Association Congress.
Grambling University Yearbook, 1969

Vaughn was a leader in building the reputation of Grambling State University in the recreation and park field. As an active member of the National Recreation and Park Association (NRPA), "Mother Pearl," as she was affectionately called by her friends and students, was an enthusiastic participant in the Society of Park and Recreation Educators and the Ethnic Minority Society.

Grambling State University, Department of Health, Physical Education, and Recreation, faculty. FIRST ROW: Mrs. Catherine Williams, Mrs. Patricia Thurston, Mrs. Bessie McKinney, Dr. C.D. Henry, Head; Miss Pearl Vaughn, Mrs. Zola Ernest SECOND ROW: Oree Banks, Virden Evans, William M. Sanders, Thomas E. Williams, Willie J. Duplantier, Fred Hobdy NOT PICTURED: Mrs. Melva Wiley, Secretary; Eddie G. Robinson.
Grambling State University Yearbook, 1964

Pearl Vaughn was the sponsor of the Recreation Club at Grambling State University in 1968.
Grambling State University Yearbook, 1968

It was through her efforts and leadership that Grambling State University hosted the first NRPA National Workshop to be convened on a historically black campus. The NRPA forum, "Careers in Parks and Recreation: The Role of the Black College and University," was held at Grambling College in Louisiana in May, 1970. It provided the first opportunity to bring together black professionals and students to discuss the problems encountered in preparing recreation professionals and paraprofessionals for careers in the recreation and park field.

Pearl Vaughn was the sponsor of the Recreation Club at Grambling State University in 1964.
Grambling State University Yearbook, 1964

SECOND ANNUAL REPORT

Improving Recreation Programs And The Quality Of Recreation Leadership In Louisiana

September 1969—June 1970

SPONSORED BY
GRAMBLING COLLEGE
and the
LOUISIANA COMMISSION ON EXTENSION AND CONTINUING EDUCATION

HEALTH, PHYSICAL EDUCATION, & RECREATION DEPARTMENT
DIVISION OF APPLIED SCIENCE AND TECHNOLOGY

GRAMBLING COLLEGE   **GRAMBLING, LA.**

One of Pearl Vaughn's publications while she was employed by Grambling State University.
Health, Physical Education, and Recreation Department, Grambling State University, Grambling, LA.

NRPA president, Sal J. Prezioso, attended the forum and proposed steps to alleviate problems concerned with career opportunities in parks and recreation for minority groups. He offered three recommendations which were unanimously accepted by the forum participants and were later passed as resolutions at the Board of Trustees meeting. These were that the Board of Trustees establish a continuing National Task Force for developing and implementing a national program to accelerate the education and training of minority group members for careers in the park and recreation field; that visitation teams be organized under the auspices and direction of the NRPA to visit, upon invitation, black universities, colleges, and junior colleges to advise and assist in the organization and development of park and recreation curricula; and that the Society of Park and Recreation Educators convene a conference of black universities, colleges, and junior colleges to develop mutually effective patterns for communication, the exchange of information, and the rendering of technical assistance.

During her tenure at Grambling College, Vaughn served as coordinator of the Recreation careers program. She was meticulous with her students, insisting on excellence and hands-on leadership experiences. She believed in and practiced the art and science of recreation leadership and community development, promoting recreation services for all people.

An example of her leadership in community development is her report "Improving Recreation Programs and the Quality of Recreation Leadership in Louisiana," published in 1970.

Over the years, accomplishments Vaughn have continued to be recognized with honors, awards, and citations. In 1992, she became the first African American to be posthumously presented the National Distinguished Pioneer Award of the Roundtable Associates, Inc. In 1996, she was one of three African-American leaders who were honored by having the book *Color of Recreation* dedicated to them.

Adapted from:

Grambling State University website. http://www.gram.edu/

National Recreation Association. (July, 1970). Black college forum gives new insight, *Parks & Recreation*. 44-45.

National Recreation and Park Ethnic Minority Siciety, Inc. (1997). *Color of recreation*. Philadelphia: Quantum Leap Publisher, Inc.

Inducted October 1988

> ***"How shall we play? Let it be with freedom, with as little regimentation as possible. Let it be expressive of fundamental, natural urges, desires, and interests of human life."***
>
> *– Lebert H. Weir*

Lebert H. Weir
1878 - 1949

As the first field representative for the National Recreation Association (1910), Lebert Howard Weir provided technical assistance to communities across the country for more than 40 years. He was the nation's foremost authority on municipal and county parks during his time. Weir's career began as a probation officer in Cincinnati, OH, where he demonstrated the importance of playgrounds in reducing juvenile delinquency. During this time, he utilized his 30-acre farm as a recreation refuge for his boys club which reached a 2,500 membership. His expertise in recreation activities was coupled with a remarkable knowledge of plant life and the outdoors. This insight enabled him to gain wide support among park administrators, behavioral experts, and natural scientists.

Weir, through his fieldwork, publications, and speeches, was a key leader in bringing together the diverse views of many park and recreation administrators. According to early park pioneers, the prime function of a park was for recreation of a "passive, semi-active kind, the dominant ideal being peaceful enjoyment amid beautiful

Lebert H. Weir, left, with Mrs. Howard Babcock, Harry Hainsworth, Buffalo's Director of Recreation.
National Recreation and Park Association Archives

surroundings of a naturalistic kind." Weir was instrumental in convincing leading park authorities to provide a broad range of recreation activities within park settings. Conversely, he was the chief spokesman and interpreter of the park movement to recreation administrators.

Weir directed a number of community recreation and park studies. Among his first studies were helping communities in California, Washington, and Oregon with assessing their needs to initiate and operate effective year-long programs. As a follow-up to the National Conference on Outdoor Recreation held in 1924, he was asked to head a major study of municipal and county park systems. This study, involving 2,700 municipalities and 40 counties, led to the publication of *Parks: A Manual of Municipal and County Parks*, which at the time was the most authoritative source of information on park management. Among Lebert Weir's other scholarly contributions were *Camping Out: A Manual of Organized Camping* and *Europe at Play*, a report on the recreational patterns of people in a number of European countries.

During World War I he helped a number of communities organize their recreation services for service men on leave. In Chillicothe, OH, he successfully strengthened and enlarged the program, raised a half-million dollars and set up a model community for recreation. This center became the national training center for War Camp Community Service workers, the forerunner of the Chicago Training Institute of the National Recreation Association.

Weir's work included service on a statewide, national and international scope. At the request of Governor John G. Winant, then chief executive of New Hampshire, he made a statewide recreation case study of that state. He also made vocational and rural recreation studies in his home state of Indiana. Weir was interested in helping to

COUNTY PARKS

County parks, the latest publication of the National Recreation Association, presents a study of county park development throughout the country, gives a picture of the material and offers a wealth of practical information. Among the subjects discussed are County Park Development, Legislation, Finance, Establishing the County Park System, Administration, Human Uses of Parks and Economic and Social Effects of County Parks. In addiction the volume contains a bibliography, a summary of legislation relation to county parks, and a summary of facts concerning county parks development in sixty-six counties. Many illustra-tions, diagrams and maps add to the interest and usefulness of the book.

Price, $2.00

NATIONAL RECREATION ASSOCIA-TION
315 Fourth Avenue, New York City

PARKS

A MANUAL OF MUNICIPAL AND COUNTY PARKS

Compiled as a result of nation-wide study of municipal and county parks conducted by the Playground and Recreation Association of America in co-operation with the American Institute of Park Executives at the request of the National Conference on Outdoor Recreation. The study was made possible through funds granted by the Laura Spelman Rockefeller Memorial.

EDITED BY L. H. WEIR

Director of the Study
Volume 1

promote and serve state consultant services in Kentucky, Indiana, Illinois, Wisconsin, and Minnesota, and in the establishment of recreation leadership courses in the institutions of higher learning in these states. He served as consultant to the National Resources Board of the Federal Government. At the invitation of the Governor of the Virgin Islands, he made studies and plans for parks and recreation in that territory.

Weir was a member of the American Recreation Society and was made a Fellow at its annual meeting in Omaha, Nebraska, in September 1948. He was also a Senior Fellow of the American Institute of Park Executives for many years. In January 1949, at the third Annual Recreation Meeting he received an "award of recognition of distinguished service in the field of recreation." Weir was again honored by his native state in October 1949, when the Indiana Municipal Park and Recreation Association presented him with a recognition plaque in absentia. In his death, November 13, 1949, the park and recreation movement lost a strong protagonist and realistic crusader who set an example of achievements which served as an inspiration to recreation leaders throughout the country.

Adapted from:

Butler, G.D. (1965). *Pioneers in public recreation*. Minneapolis, MN: Burgess Publishing Company.
National Recreation Association (December, 1949). "Lebert H. Weir." *Recreation*. New York.

Inducted October 1999

" *The national park system exists for the benefit of all the people, and it must be so managed that its natural and historic values will be available, let us say in the year 2066, when Joe Doaks and Agnes Hobbleskirt will be born. Such is the responsibility of the service, or, if you prefer, the bureaucrats.* "

–Conrad L. Wirth

Conrad L. Wirth
1899-1993

Conrad "Connie" Louis Wirth, born in Elizabeth Park, Hartford, CT. was the son of Theodore and Leonie Mense Wirth. Theodore Wirth, well-known superintendent of municipal parks, instilled a lifelong passion for parks in his second of three sons. In 1923 Conrad Wirth earned a Bachelor of Science degree in architecture and landscape planning from Massachusetts Agricultural College (University of Massachusetts). For the next five years, Wirth went into private practice in New Orleans and San Francisco as a landscape and town planner.

In 1928 Wirth joined the National Park and Planning Commission in Washington, which was the start of his long federal career. Horace Albright brought him to the National Park Service (NPS) in 1931 as assistant director for land planning. When President Roosevelt launched his public works programs, Albright was responsible for implementing it as part of the Interior Department. Albright delegated that responsibility to Wirth and in 1933 he was given supervisory responsibility for all state and county park activities of the Civilian Conservation Corps (CCC).

Wirth with CCC Director Robert Fechner.
National Park Service Historic Photograph Collection

During the Great Depression, Wirth distinguished himself with his brilliant implementation of CCC programs in support of federal, state, and local parks. He developed proposals for creating new state parks, and he oversaw the planning, design, and construction of the facilities necessary for parks to accommodate public use. Under his direction, the NPS employed hundreds of thousands of CCC workers to construct roads, trails, cabins, museums, campgrounds, picnic grounds, administration offices, and other state park facilities. Wirth was also a member of the committee that founded and established "Shangri La," now known as Camp David[1], a retreat that every President since Franklin Delano Roosevelt has utilized. The National Geographic Society cited Wirth for his contribution to the welfare of the country as director of the CCC.

Wirth's remarkable contributions in this role were a prelude to the profound impact he had on the NPS when subsequently serving as the agency's director from 1951 to 1964. NPS director, Arthur E. Demaray, named

Conrad Wirth was the director of the National Park Service from 1951-1964.
National Park Service Historic Photograph Collection

---

[1] Camp David was originally built as a camp for federal government employees and their families by the Works Progress Administration, starting in 1935 opening in 1938. In 1942 it was converted to a presidential retreat by President Franklin D. Roosevelt.

Conrad Wirth on shore of St. Mary Lake, Glacier National Park, June 1960.
National Park Service Historic Photograph Collection

Wirth an associate director in 1951. Soon thereafter Wirth succeeded Demaray. In some ways this was an unusual appointment because Wirth had no experience in the field, but he had proven his administrative ability in the headquarters office. A planner and developer at heart, Wirth moved in a different direction from earlier NPS preservationist policies. Wirth was confronted with parks that had deteriorated during the war years when their general maintenance and upkeep was suspended.

After the war, when gas rationing was removed, millions of Americans poured into the parks. Their infrastructure was inadequate to accommodate these visitors. Wirth proposed an ambitious development program to commemorate the 50th anniversary of the establishment of the NPS, and, in his own words, to "overcome the inroads of neglect and to restore to the American people a National Park System

adequate for their needs." The goal was to bring all units of the NPS "up to a consistently high standard of preservation, staffing, and physical development, and to consolidate them fully into one national park system."

The scale of Wirth's vision was extraordinary. There had been little investment in the parks after the war, and Wirth believed the only way to quantumly increase it was to present a total program for the whole system from which all legislation and their constituents would benefit, rather than to seek incremental improvements in particular parks each year. Such an ambitious plan would require a level of annual appropriations many times higher than the existing level. Titled Mission 66, the ten-year construction and rehabilitation program cost $11 billion. Wirth personally convinced President Eisenhower of the merits of the plan, carefully cultivated

Conrad L. Wirth at Dedication, Death Valley Visitor Center, November 12, 1960.
National Park Service Historic Photograph Collection

powerful people in Congress, and ensured there was something nice in the package for every member of the House and Senate who had a park in their district. No legislation authorizing Mission 66 was passed rather it relied on annual appropriations. Congress followed through with these appropriations and Mission 66 resulted in the major upgrading of visitor centers, roads, trails, and other park amenities. The success of the program stimulated the creation of the Outdoor Recreation Resource Review Commission in 1958.

Wirth's leadership was influential in the development and organization of numerous groups. His philosophy and approach to public service is best captured in his biography *Parks, Politics, and the People*. He was an active member and president of

the American Institute of Park Executives, executive director of the Hudson Valley Commission, helped organize and served as a board member for the White House Historical Society, first chairman of the New York State Historic Trust, and a trustee emeritus for the National Geographic Society. In 1965 his diplomacy skills and field experience played an instrumental role in the merging of several professional organizations to form the National Recreation and Park Association.

A renowned conservationist and manager of outdoor recreation resources, Wirth's career spanned a period of more than 50 years, 33 of which were spent with the National Park Service. Numerous awards and recognitions were presented to him during his career. Among

Wirth Environmental Award developed by National Park Foundation for the century of leadership provided by Theodore and Conrad Wirth.
Parks and Recreation, July 1986

them were two Pugsley Gold Medals from the American Scenic and Historic Preservation Society, Theodore Roosevelt Medal, Rockefeller Public Service Award, Conservation Award of the American Forestry Association, and the Everly Gold Medal of the American Institute of Park Executives. He was particularly proud of the Wirth Environmental Award, which the National Park Foundation named for him and his father. Wirth was the first recipient of this award for his efforts to preserve the nation's open land and waters. His legacy will forever be etched in the landscape of our nation's parks.

Adapted from:

American Academy of Park and Recreation Administration. (1983). *Legends of the American Park and Recreation Association* Downloaded on May 10, 2008 from http://www.aapra.org/legends.html

Crompton, J.L. (in press). *Twentieth century champions of parks and conservation: The Pugsley Award Recipients 1928-1964. Volume I.* Champaign, IL: Sagamore Publishing.

Saxon, W. (July 28, 1993). Conrad L. Wirth, 93; Led National Parks Service, *The New York Times.*

Inducted October 1988

> *" Parks are for the people. "*
>
> *–Theodore Wirth*

Theodore Wirth

1863-1949

Theodore Wirth, a Swiss landscape gardener, became widely recognized in the beginning of the twentieth century as the dean of the park movement in America. While serving as superintendent of parks in Hartford, CT, he developed the first municipal rose garden in the nation, and thereby set a standard for emerging park departments to follow.

His greatest accomplishments in the park field occurred while he was superintendent of the Minneapolis Park Department. Under Wirth's direction, the Minneapolis system, developed around its chain of lakes, became widely acclaimed. His ambition was to make the Minneapolis park system unequaled in the country with its natural majesty and recreation opportunities. A true love for the grace of nature and landscape, coupled with skill in the horticultural adornment of land in both formal and informal gardens, enabled Wirth to develop and advance park philosophy in America.

While initially a follower of the old school park concept—parks should be established

Theodore Wirth House; constructed in 1910 by the Minneapolis Board of Park Commissioners to lure Wirth to Minneapolis.
Minneapolis Park Legacy Society

first for beauty and aesthetic dignity and secondly for passive recreation—Wirth soon become a strong proponent for the establishment of playgrounds and the use of parks for active forms of recreation.

Wirth was a founding member of the American Institute of Park Executives in 1898. He passed his commitment to parks and to the environment on to his family. Two of his sons (Conrad and Walter Wirth)

Commissioners and officials planting trees at Lake Calhoun in 1916. This was part of the development for the Minneapolis Parkway System. Commissioner R. E. Fischer; J. A. Ridgeway, Secretary of the Board; Commissioners Harry B. Cramer, Joseph Allen, P. C. Deming; Attorney C. J. Rockwood; Commissioners W. F. Decker, A. A. McRae, Francis A. Gross; and Theodore Wirth, Superintendent of Parks.
Minneapolis Park Legacy Society

First Municipal Rose Garden in Elizabeth Park, Hartford, CT, early 1900s.
Hartford History Center, Hartford Public Library

and a grandson (Theodore J. Wirth) have maintained his heritage of service to the park movement. The National Park Foundation established the Wirth Environmental Award to honor the century of leadership provided by Wirth and his son, Conrad, who served as director of the National Park Service for many years.

Wirth's philosophy of park use was that the parks are for the people. Under his direction of the system "keep off the grass" signs disappeared from Minneapolis parks, and he introduced playgrounds and other features of park utilities suitable for the intensive use to which municipal park systems are put. Horticultural advancement in park work was one of his aims.

One of the most important principles to which Wirth adhered in his park administration work is that the expense of facilities for any special interest, such as golf, together with the cost of operation and maintenance, should be met by those who participate in these specialized forms of recreation. He also insisted that no service in parks should be conducted for private gain, and remained opposed to concessions in parks. He advocated that refectories, boat, and other revenue-producing facilities be operated by the park department in the interest of the public.

A pioneer in many phases of planning, Wirth was one of the first to advocate beauty along highways. He emphasized the importance of roadside improvement

Theodore Wirth received the Pugsley Medal in 1930 "for his services in developing the Minneapolis Park System." The Pugsley Medal is the most prestigious award that recognizes outstanding contributions to the promotion and development of public parks in the United States.
Minneapolis Park Legacy Society

from the standpoint of appearance. This influenced greatly how local, state, and federal agencies viewed the significance of their natural resources.

Wirth brought fame to himself, as well as to Minneapolis, through his park work, and he received high honors as a park planner and executive. Minneapolis Parks were rated number one in the nation by 1928. Their distinguishing feature, a chain of lakes within the city limits, each surrounded by park property, is a worthy memorial to his work and vision.

Adapted from:

Wirth, T. (2006 Limited Edition). *Minneapolis Park System 1883-1944*. Minneapolis, MN: Minneapolis Park Legacy Society.

EPILOGUE

History is the witness that testifies to the passing of time; it illumines reality, vitalizes memory, provides guidance in daily life and brings us tidings of antiquity.
Cicero, *Pro Publio Sestio*, (106 B.C. - 43 B.C.)

Over the four decades in which I have worked within a college or university setting, I have witnessed younger generations becoming disconnected from much of what has gone before. The members of these contemporary generations have lost their history and, unfortunately, their interest in that history. As the various generations —Generation X, Generation Y, Generation Now, and Generation Me—have succeeded one another there has been an increasing focus on the present with less interest in the past.

Historians have argued that disconnection from prior generations has been a concern throughout history. However, I believe that lack of connection is increasing in pace with each ensuing generation. It could be the rapid pace of technological change that makes present generations less aware and less appreciative of life in prior generations. It could be the simple overwhelming flood of information that is increasingly available to present generations who are more interested in a sound bite. It could be our withdrawal from oral traditions passed from one generation to another that has made history and the people of history to be of lesser importance.

As a youth growing up in Minnesota in the 1960s, I was intrigued with the number of parks, parkways, trails, streets and roads named for Theodore Wirth. Each seemed to be a wonderful destination or to lead a visitor to that desired destination. At that same time Conrad Wirth was director of the National Park Service providing a living link to the legacy of a family dedicated to the park and recreation movement in America. During that time, I worked in the Minnesota State Park system and attended meetings at which Udert "Judge" Hella told stories of his friendship with members of the Wirth family and of the value of parks in service to the residents and visitors to Minnesota. He instilled in me a sense of responsibility to the environment, to those who had worked diligently for parks, to those who enjoyed the results of that work, and to the land. Judge Hella recognized and shared the legacy of Theodore and Conrad Wirth, members of the Recreation and Park Hall of Fame. In turn, Judge Hella was a recipient of another valued recognition in the profession, the Pugsley Award, as were Theodore and Conrad Wirth. Each in his own way made outstanding and lasting contributions to public parks in America. Each in his own way influenced my life and my decision to become a professional in parks and recreation.

While I was influenced by members of the Recreation and Park Hall of Fame early in my life, that influence has continued daily since then. What can we learn today from someone who worked during the last century? Much—and in ways that can impact the current delivery of park and recreation services. These members of the Hall of Fame faced many of the same issues and daily challenges that face the profession today.

Frederick Law Olmsted observed urban crowding and unhealthy lifestyles of those living in New York City. His Greensward plan for Central Park transformed a swamp into the most valuable real estate in the world. This urban development literally moved a city as New York City expanded to surround Central Park. Jane Addams and Joseph Lee observed similar conditions in their communities and cities, but chose to address the crowding and health issues through programs rather than urban planning. Each addressed problems that existed in their day and continue to exist today.

Dorothy Enderis observed the plight of youth in Milwaukee particularly in pre-school and after-school hours. Her intervention with recreation programs solved a local problem that is easily identified in many communities today. Inner city, at-risk youth continue to need the foundation of services championed by Dorothy Enderis and found to be of great value in changing a community.

William Penn Mott worked in an era of budget cuts, employment freezes, and reduced revenue under Governor Reagan. Yet it was the limitation of easy resources that stimulated some of the most creative ideas from Mott and his staff. This creativity continues to benefit the San Francisco Bay area, the state of California, and the National Park Service.

Garrett Eppley, Charles Brightbill, Harold Meyer, and Edith Ball all worked in academic settings addressing the traditional missions of colleges and universities for research, teaching, and services. Each succeeded in balancing those roles.

These individuals represent different aspects of the field and had different, yet significant, impacts. The individuals illustrated above and in this book each creatively intervened in existing conditions to better the lives of those in the community. We can easily identify with limited revenue, budget cuts, and employment freezes, but can also easily identify with the creative, professional responses of these members of the Hall of Fame. Each left a legacy of knowledge, service, and impact on lives that serve as goals for educators, professionals, and citizens today.

Each of the individuals chronicled in the Recreation and Park Hall of Fame has achieved the criteria detailed by Cicero. Each has been a witness to the passing of time, but has also utilized that time to inspire others, preserve the best of what they encountered, and enrich the lives of their contemporaries and in doing so, enriched the lives of those of us who have followed. As such, each of these individuals made history. They faced challenges and concerns with ingenuity, creativity, and passion. As innovators and leaders in the profession, they regularly invented solutions to those problems. We can draw on that knowledge, creativity, passion, and those solutions to resolve the challenges in our lives and in our profession. These members of the Hall of Fame have illumined reality for their contemporaries and for us. They saw the circumstances, often dire, of those around them and worked to improve the settings and the lives of citizens. As lights in dark places, each member brightened the future with the legacy of their work. Their lights still shine brightly years after their direct service has ended.

Agnes Repplier wrote, "It is in his pleasure that a man really lives; it is from his leisure that he constructs the true fabric of self." Through their respective and corporate legacy, these individuals provided pleasure for many. The parks and recreation experiences these individuals labored to provide for others became the leisure from which many constructed the true fabric of self. From that fabric, a society and nation was formed yielding a culture in which a profession like parks and recreation could grow and develop. Do the recreation experiences of people matter today? Is leisure really an important aspect of life? Is the provision of parks and recreation an essential service? These members of the Hall of Fame built individual lives and entire communities on a foundation of parks, recreation, and leisure and left their world better because of that foundation.

The Hall of Fame brings us tidings of antiquity. It was Confucius who stated, "I am not one who was born in the possession of knowledge;

141

I am one who is fond of antiquity, and earnest in seeking it there." If Confucius could assert the value of the tidings of antiquity and the knowledge available there, how much more can we gain by earnestly seeking knowledge from those who have gone before?

These profiles in leadership for parks and recreation should produce a fondness for history, its reality, and its memory. Those who are profiled possessed much knowledge and passion. We should earnestly seek that knowledge and passion with the intent of letting it provide guidance for our daily professional lives.

Lowell Caneday, Ph.D.
Professor, Oklahoma State University
Chair, Hall of Fame Committee